MW01070466

"18 Wheels and Jesus"

All Scripture, unless otherwise indicated, is taken from the King James translation of the bible.

ISBN-13: 978-1508626602
ISBN-10: 150862660X

Printed in the United States of America

Author: Hulse, Jerry Wayne
Contributing Author: Robert Hale

Cover & Editor: Destiny Management

Title **"18 Wheels and Jesus "**

Sub Title: **"Trucking for the Cross "**

Total Pages: 107

Category - Drama

Non-Fiction – Self-help / inspiration / religion

Religion – Christian philosophy

Bible (Quotations) Christian Literature (Quotations)

Content Rating: General (G) reading suitable for all ages.

A Statement from the Author

There is a revival on the highways and byways of America and around the world which prompted the writing of this novel. It is a known fact that the Trucking Ministry is the world's largest mission field (estimated at over 70 million people) of which some have given over their lives to being a part of God's kingdom because of witnesses like the one mentioned in this novel. We decided to write this as a fictional novel in order to experience what it would be like to be in one of the 18 wheelers and be a preacher in today's society. One soldier that we will call Paul (The Preacher) is that person and we will pretend that he is known throughout the trucking industry that we might gain some insight as to what it would be like to actually be a part of this ministry. We will get to ride along and experience the ups and downs in this man of God's life as he is used of God to touch truckers, dockworkers, policemen and many souls everywhere he goes. The living God has allowed his ministry to travel around the world by means of videos and audiocassettes. His CB handle "The Preacher" is recognized nationwide as he has devoted his life to reach the lost at any cost. The Preacher in this novel has been involved in television and pioneered several radio programs. His ministering has been done on a one to one basis. He ministers where God manifests Himself.

People have witnessed, on several occasions, the Holy Spirit drawing the Preacher to someone who needed a personal touch or a word from God. The Preacher always believed and practiced that God's work done God's way would never lack for resources.

This novel is written that Christ may receive the glory and not man for he is worthy to be praised! I (Little Silas) begin this novel with The Preacher and I having a lunch break at the Petro truck Stop in Bordentown, NJ. The Preacher and I had just entered the restaurant area of the truck stop and were politely seated by the waitress. We were having a conversation about people with a zeal for the work of God when the subject came up about General George Patton's faith and divine design; It is well known that General Patton had a reputation of being a rough individual. When I wondered why the subject had been brought up, the Preacher replied with a gleam in his eye, "I'll tell you why, they had to run Patton out of gas to stop him, and otherwise he would go and would not quit 'till he got the job done. That's like some churches now; they wouldn't give anyone gas if they have messed up even once. That's why God has sent His people like us out here giving the gas!" We finished our meal and began walking around on the convenience side of the restaurant when the Preacher was suddenly drawn like a magnet to an individual. He introduced himself, "Hi, I'm Paul; you might know me better by my CB handle "The Preacher". The elderly driver replied, "Hi...yea I've heard of you. They call me "The General" on the CB, 'cause my last name is Patton." The Holy Spirit was confirming that Paul needed to minister to this driver. We were blessed a few months later; by the General giving us a great witness of answered prayers.

That night Brother Patton received the baptism of the Holy Ghost. I started driving tractor-trailers in 1994 full–time. The Preacher was actively ministering in the same company I worked for. Since the first time he prayed for me, various blessings of the LORD have manifested themselves in my life.

Many miracles had already happened, but they seemed to accelerate after he had spoken a blessing upon me.

I had wrestled with a stumbling block for years and within a few months after the anointing of God, through The Preacher, had instructed me on the essence of breaking generational curses; I was freed and won the victory.

"Eighteen Wheels and Jesus"

Preface: The Nightmare Eases

Preface

The Nightmare Eases

After a revival meeting in October of 2001, The Preacher felt as if all hell had broken loose upon his life. The battle may have ensued due to the fact that he was being moved to complete a work of his life's story. He knew he was living in the days when the love of many had waxed cold and churches were more interested in themselves than the culture around them. The Preacher had been told that a demonic curse was spoken against him during this particular revival meeting. It seemed as if it was true. Depression is hard, but oppression is worse. This novel is designed to build faith and courage that will lift us up when everything seems to be going wrong so we may once again stand and fight the fight of faith against an enemy that is determined to demise our destruction.

LORD, we thank you for the very light of your WORD in our times of trial and distress!

Romans 8:28

"And we know that all things work together for good to them that love God, to them who are the called according to His purpose"

The Preacher believed this persecution was brought about to turn a search light on in the deep regresses of his spirit. He needed to remove his personal pride, and he felt unworthy of God's Grace at the time.

He learned to abhor any pocket of hidden darkness that appears within his spirit. His blessed revelations from God occurred when He lifted only a small portion of his covering of grace. The Preacher in this novel now understands that it is God who can be trusted, and not our self.

Romans 1:17

"For therein is the righteousness of God revealed from faith to faith: as it is written, the just shall live by faith"

We believe that God is soon to move on little "David's" to take the lambs out of the mouth of demonic roaring "lions". Challenging Satan in his own territory with the God given authority of His glorious body of power through the Holy Spirit will defeat him. Our hope and prayer is that God will bless you, protect you, and open your eyes as a result of this novel. We read in God's word that Jesus Christ was manifested in the flesh to destroy the work of Satan and his demons. Through Christ's victory we have victory. We have power and authority in the name of The LORD Jesus Christ according to His WORD! He cannot lie. Jesus told us to seek first the kingdom of God and His righteousness and all these things will be added unto us.

Like The Preacher in this novel, if we seek the mind of The Spirit, the Spirit of Holiness and Truth (which is God's kingdom) and do so with an upright heart, He will not withhold any good thing from us!

Psalm 84:11

"For The LORD GOD is a sun and a shield: The LORD will give grace and glory: no good thing will He withhold from them that walk uprightly"

In the book of Jude we are told that Michael, the archangel of God, did not scream and yell at the demonic spirit he fought against. He simply spoke, *"The LORD rebuke thee."*

Jude 1:9

"Yet Michael the archangel, when contending with the devil he disputed about the body of Moses, durst not bring him a railing accusation, but said, The LORD rebuke thee."

Victory was given because of the authority given to Michael in his position and in his relationship with the Lord. Satan had not yet been totally defeated, now he has! How much greater is our relationship with The Father! Through the relationship of adoption, we are sons & daughters: the very siblings of Jesus himself. Satan's main tool is deception and like a magician, smoke and mirrors are his tools. He keeps your eyes and thoughts occupied with one hand while the other hand is working to deceive. His main entertainment is to "...steal, kill, and to destroy." His hope is that you will not look at the "big picture" and see the obvious end result is that of disaster. If you will - look beyond the lies.........

1st Peter 5:8

"Be sober, be vigilant, for your adversary the devil, as a roaring lion, walketh about, seeking whom he may devour:"

DELIVERANCE
(On the Road)

Paul, the Preacher pulled onto a certified truck scale at the "76" truck stop on I-20 and was told by the fuel clerk that the scale's computer was not reading. After parking his rig, Paul told the clerk he would be at the chapel until they figured out the source of the malfunction. The clerk told him it was a rare occurrence and she would wait a few minutes to try again. The moment his foot touched the first step, at the door of the trucker's chapel, he heard the voice of the HOLY GHOST say, "I want you to pray for someone to be delivered from demons of alcohol today."

The Preacher felt in his spirit this ministering was imminent and he proceeded into the chapel with his heart and spirit girded to do battle. The Chaplain greeted him inside and Paul declared the Word of The LORD that had been given to him. The Chaplain informed him that there were five other ministers, at that moment, in the truck stop's restaurant dealing with a young man who had that very problem! Suddenly, Paul was startled as the chapel doors opened and in came a procession of ministers, accompanying a young man who fit the stereotype of an alcoholic, smell and all.

The clergymen told him that God had moved separately on each of their hearts to minister at this truck stop and that they were led to this tormented individual. The young man had refused to thus far. They were frustrated and wanted Paul to minister to the man because they were familiar with his reputation. Paul walked over to the young man, empowered by the WORD of The LORD spoken to him, he fired off: "Young man! God has gone to a lot of trouble for you! He has even broken a certified scale to get me in here! Five area preachers here too! Just for you!

He is so concerned over you young man and you act like you don't care!!! You're wasting their time and mine! Tearing up a scale where I can't even get weighed...JUST FOR YOUR SOUL.... AND YOU WON'T RESPOND!!! Let me tell you what you need to do, right now! If you aren't going to respond to God's call, and bow to His authority, you better go drink all the water you can drink! 'Cause there isn't going to be any water where you're headed!" The Spirit moved on that boy! He broke and said, "Preacher...pray for me." Paul took his hand to pray and a great move of The SPIRIT of CHRIST manifested in him, so much that he broke out in chills and goose bumps of sweat. Paul intensely sense the presence of the demonic force gripping the young man.

It continued to the point that Paul called out, "Devil..." with confidence of the anointing on and in him, "...you heard him say with his own spirit that he want to be free! He wants God's salvation offered through God's Son JESUS CHRIST. Now devil...I don't think you want to argue with this!" A sigh of relief passed over the young man as he was delivered. Then the glow of God's glory appeared on his face as he exclaimed, "Preacher, I feel clean!" Mini-revival broke out in the little trailer chapel, as they all rejoiced over what God had done in this young man's life!

Paul found himself amazed when he got to his truck and the scale was now working. He reflected on the way The LORD had temporarily broken a certified scale to save and deliver a precious soul. He's always amazed at God's awesome way, the added value God places upon a soul who will either be with him in eternity or be separated from his presence for ever and cast into the lake of fire on that great day when all will stand before him and give an account of their life lived here on earth.

2nd Peter 3:9

"The Lord is not slack concerning His promise, but is longsuffering to us-ward, not willing that any should perish, but that all should come to repentance."

Turning The Page

(The early childhood years)

Paul can still remember his father calling for everyone to gather at the living room sofa before bedtime where each night the family would kneel to pray. Paul knew what kneeling was, but to pray was a different matter. His maternal grandfather lived nearby and he was a prominent Methodist preacher in the area; Rev. Grace. When he was older, Paul began attending church with his papaw and his grandmother (Rose).

It took only a few visits for him to fall in love with God's children, and the attention he received as the pastor's grandson was especially delightful. The first place Paul remembers realizing he had been blessed with a photographic memory was in Mrs. Attention's' Sunday school class. The children were instructed to learn the books of the bible. Paul was able to recite them with ease and perfection, without having to study. The gold stars and extra attention definitely contributed to his enjoyment of Sunday school and to this day, he can still recall the gentle voice of his grandmother asking him if he would like to attend church with her. Paul loved being in the class and he loved church.

One day, his grandfather taught him three cords on a guitar. With the blessing of a photographic memory, he learned the cords, made up a song, and played lead guitar with his grandfather playing rhythm, all in the same day. Paul was fascinated to realize that when his grandfather preached, he was able to easily follow the scripture and read ahead as the message developed. The WORD seemed to jump out at him and he generally knew what the next point would be.

He was able to discern what the points would be before they were even preached. Paul did not understand this gift but it gave him a burning desire to know The God of the Bible.

He remembers walking along the breezeway at his house and asking, "God, if you are real, where are you? I want you to reveal yourself to me. I love you so much! I need to get to know you." He expected a whirlwind or a physical manifestation of some kind but nothing happened. It wasn't long, however, before his life began to change. One night, while lying in the bed, he reflected on his grandfather's preaching so emotionally and with such vigor that he was dripping sweat by the end of the sermon. Paul reread the text of the sermon, the seventeenth chapter of the book of Revelation.

Revelation 17:9-10

"And here is the mind which hath wisdom. The even heads are seven mountains, on which the woman sitteth. And there are seven kings: five are fallen, and one is, and the other is not yet come; and when he cometh, he must continue a short space."

1st Samuel 3:4

"That the LORD called Samuel: and he answered, Here am I."

Paul heard a voice say, "That is Rome, Italy." He turned to see who had spoken but he was alone. He was about eight years old at the time and did not know what or where Rome, Italy was! Paul realized he had his first supernatural experience with the Spirit of God.. He felt a burden for more, and promised God to be a minister like his grandfather, if he would continue to be blessed with such experiences. It was not long thereafter that the Sprit of God began to manifest these supernatural occurrences and things started to happen with some frequency.

Paul was in prayer by his bedside one night with his Bible open when he asked God to reveal Himself to him. He knew that "voice" had been instructing him for some time on teachings in the Bible. Suddenly, his Bible pages began to turn by themselves.

It was as if someone had wet their thumb, turning the pages with an unseen hand. All the doors and windows to his room were already closed. There was no mechanical air on either. It frightened him so bad that he cried and begged whatever was doing this to please stop. God honored his request and stopped the Bible pages from turning, but the supernatural gifts also stopped for a long period of time.

Jeremiah 1:4&5

Then the word of the LORD came unto me, saying, Before I formed thee in the belly I knew thee; and before thou came forth out of the womb I sanctified thee, and I ordained thee a prophet unto the nations.

Paul then devoted his spare time in learning new cords on his guitar and became involved with other students in school to start up a rock and roll band. He would occasionally attend church services out of respect for his grandfather but there was a tension in him pulling him toward the worldly life style. This finally drove a wedge between him and his earthly father. It was during this time that Paul's father had announced his call into the ministry and later became a pastor of a small church in Somewhere, Tennessee. Feeling that he no longer had the love of his father, Paul turned to local gangs for their security and Support.

Many young teens today turn to the gangs for security and protection. The gang has provided a type of false security and hope that should be found in a family. God still had his hand upon this wayward boy and would bring him into the plan that he had for his life and ministry.

The Moving of the Water
(On the Road and at home)

While driving his truck to eastern Virginia late one night, Paul was musing on God's greatness. He had prayed earlier in the week for the money to purchase a Thompson-Chain reference Bible with index tabs. Paul fully believed that God would answer this prayer! His ministry was televised and broadcast on several radio stations but his ministry did not have extra cash. His focus turned to a conversation beginning on the CB radio. A driver commented that he had been suffering from migraine headaches for weeks and doctors had been unable to help him. Paul keyed his mike and said, "Driver, I know a doctor that can cure you." He said, "Oh yeah, who!" Paul requested they turn to another channel to keep from disturbing the other drivers. He began building the hurting man's faith by discussing the ways God had been moving in his life then asked if he could pray for him. A few minutes after he prayed, the driver keyed his mike and said, "hey Preacher, what kind of God do you serve? I been to all kind of doctors, spent all kind of money, and none of them could help me. But now my headache is gone!" Paul smiled and keyed back, "Let's go up here to the truck stop and I'll introduce you to him." Paul was blessed to win this driver to the LORD in the rain-drenched parking lot of the "T/A" in Ashland, VA. They both rejoiced, kicking puddles like school children on the way into the restaurant. Once inside, Paul received a phone call that a Bible had been found by the side of the road lying in a puddle of water. Paul questioned the caller on the details of the Bible. It was the exact one he had asked God for. No one except God knew about his prayer for the Bible. When he arrived home and began to look through it, there was one spot highlighted, where the marker ribbon was placed that had long been his private verse with God.

God had given this verse to Paul years before as a precursor to his miracle-healing ministry which later became the basis of a great soul winning ministry. Paul had found that different bible scholars referred to this particular scripture as that of a miracle healing ministry. The scripture can be found in the book of Matthew. A man was in the temple and had a withered hand. The verse shows the power of God on display stretching out to set the captives free. This is a type of person full of the Spirit and power of God being used by the Lord in special services to set the people free by being called into the miracle ministry.

Matthew 12: 13

Then saith he to the man, stretch forth thy hand, And he stretched it forth: and it was whole like as the other.

Playing The Game

(The latter childhood years)

Without God's voice or supernatural occurrences in Paul's life, he soon forgot the miracles God had blessed him with. Church became a game to him. Like most children, Paul thrived on attention. Whenever his grandfather gave the invitation to receive salvation, he was always the first to come forward. From time to time, when being questioned, he would simply agree with whatever his grandfather would say and pretend he understood (what it was to be saved).

He thought it was all a game adults liked to play too. He would bow and pretend to pray as the elders gathered around him. He would wait till he thought everyone was ready, then he would stand up and all would rejoice together, as if a game. The day came when he truly desired to be saved, but he couldn't find the help he needed. He had played the game too long and far too well.

Genesis 8:21

"...for the imagination of man's heart is evil from his youth..."

During these years of religious effort, Paul occasionally sensed the presence of the Holy Spirit. He sang and played the guitar during church services for his grandfather. He remembers God blessing the singing services. Once when he sang a favorite song of his papaw; "The Pearly White City", the service had to come to a stop as a young man came forward to receive Jesus Christ as LORD and Savior. God had revealed Jesus to a lost soul through a child who had not yet reached the age of accountability. Paul can still remember shouting and praising the LORD during some of these events. People would comment, "He's just God happy."

Then evil came in the form of temptation to steal his shout and replace it with a cloud of shame. After coming into his teen years, Paul quit playing the religious scene. The Blessing of his musical ability became a curse allowing him access to places in Satan's realm. His church teachings began to fade away as he became more interested in playing music in bars, then known as honkytonks.

Paul realized that when he played the music, it was as if it was not him, instead, an unseen force trying to control his body movements. Paul would actually get lost in his music and he also greatly enjoyed the attention musicians received from women.

A Holiday In Heaven

(On The Road)

One of Paul's fondest memories of the miraculous working of God through him for others was while driving across Georgia and deciding to stop at the 76 truck stop in Ringgold, GA. The next day was payday and he had $27.00 in his wallet so he decided to splurge on a steak for dinner. Paul had been trained in martial arts and this taught him to be aware of his surroundings at all times. God uses our past training to accent parts of our ministry life in the present. He noticed a beautiful blue Western Star truck decorated with Bible verses, crosses, and bumper stickers. They were all neatly placed in order for the Glory of God. He also noticed a couple of cars on the backside of the lot with several families standing in the area. It is common practice for people who clean and polish trucks to camp out at the warmer weather truck stops but with his limited finances, he had no reason to approach them. It is fascinating how God can take natural circumstances and turn them into supernatural ones! Paul had just left the restaurant and was headed for his truck and barely noticed a teenage boy rapidly approaching. The young man asked Paul for money for both himself and his mother, stating that they had spent everything they had to repair their vehicle. Paul said, "Son, if I had known that, I wouldn't have eaten that big meal just a moment ago. You probably saw me coming out of the restaurant with a toothpick in my mouth waddling like a plumb turkey ready to be butchered. All I got is $7.00 to my name!" The young man looked at Paul sadly but did not reply. Paul continued, "I am a Christian though, and I believe if we pray we can see God move! Let's go talk to your mom." After talking to them both and praying, Paul was lead by the Holy Spirit to talk with the driver in the blue gospel truck.

The Holy Spirit stopped him on the way to the truck, instructing him to open his wallet and ask the teenager to count the $1.00 dollar bills. "One, two, three" putting each bill into the boy's hand and showing him the now empty wallet without knowing why. Paul, said "I am willing to give all that I have, but maybe this other driver can help too." He introduced himself to the driver, stating that he was a Christian also, and asked for help with the situation. He explained the details to this true man of God. The driver's first response was to pray. He suggested they contact other drivers on the CB radio to ask for help. Paul stated he had given all he had and pulled out his wallet to demonstrate and the teenager started to scream! His wallet now contained $32.00! The boy said, "You don't understand mister, he just made me count his money and look in his wallet!! All he had was $7.00 and nothing else!" The other driver was not surprised and began praising God, and then he proceeded to help gather helping funds from all over the lot by testifying on the CB radio. The young man gave his life to Christ and vowed that he too wanted to preach the gospel. This caused joy in heaven around the throne of God and Heaven went on a holiday rejoicing over this one who was rescued from the enemy's camp.

Paul then left Ringgold, Georgia and proceeded westward across I-24 to the top of Mount Eagle, TN. This mountain's reputation for the death of many truck drivers is well known. The grades are difficult to handle and drivers usually adjust their brakes before descending, especially if they do not have an engine braking system. Paul stopped to check his own brakes, there was a small group of gospel singers, The Trucking Troubadours, snapping photos of their excursion for future advertisements.

Paul had known these Troubadours out west and had supported their ministry. Paul reintroduced himself and the driver expressed to him that he had deep reservations about adjusting his brakes on their tractor-trailer because he was not familiar with the system. He glorified in the LORD for providing a certified mechanic, as well as truck driver, to come to the aid of His children during their time of need. He adjusted their brakes and was blessed to meet this group several more times in Texas. Paul adventures as a long haul truck driver allowed him to meet several of the different ministries that were on the road ministering to the truckers at various truck stops. One of his favorite sayings is to bloom here you are planted and being used.

This particular singing group became wonderful friends with him during these excursions. Paul remembers another group called Trucking for Jesus that had their own tractor and mobil trailer that was converted into a mini chapel for services wherever they were allowed to set up. They were out of Virginia and once a year they would start on their missionary trip to the west coast and work their way back home stopping at truck stops that they might be instruments of the Lord to help change lives. Paul expressed his gratitude to them being used of the Lord to influence his life.

The Heart Condition

Proverbs 12:25

"Heaviness in the heart of man maketh it stoop: but a good word maketh it glad."

When Paul was in his early twenties, his cardiologist informed him an operation was necessary due to fluid buildup around his heart that could only be removed by surgery. It was literally squeezing the life out of him by making his heart too heavy. His EKG was erratic. The operation was to take place the following Monday, but on Sunday, he was coednsu with uncertainty and felt he should take his fears to church. Brother Faith was the Pastor of a small church in Somewhere, TN.

Over the years, Paul had seen countless people receive salvation under his grandfather's ministry. During this service however, he received a clear understanding of the gospel and the free gift of Jesus Christ for the first time in his life.

Romans 5:15-18

"But not as the offence, so also is the free gift. For if through the offence of one many be dead, much more the grace of God, and the gift by grace, which is by one man, Jesus Christ, hath abounded unto many."

The Spirit of GOD moved on Paul to open the special package of God's gift of love for him, and he was born into the Kingdom of GOD". The next day, his physician ran a few more tests before the operation and he was sent home without operating, His EKG was now normal. God had cured both of Paul's heart conditions on the same day!

Shortly afterwards Paul's father went to Pastor Faith's place of employment to thank him for leading his wayward son to Christ. The "game" that Paul had been playing up to this time had been a horrible nightmare for those who loved him. It didn't take long for Paul to develop a hunger for the word of God. He devoted every spare moment he had to memorizing the scriptures and talking with the Lord about the call and plan he had for his life. The Lord began to work with Paul to bring him into his ministry calling.

An Angel to Pray For

(On The Road)

Quiet time with the LORD on the road was some of the best times in Paul's life. God spoke to him while on a run informing him that he needed to pray for an Angel to be delivered. At the time, Paul did not understand what God's message meant. His satellite communication device had beeped to signal a routing change that would take him off his regular route by several miles. The new route led near a town in Kentucky he was familiar with. He had a friend who had been making headway in ministry in this town so he called him and they met. During the conversation, Paul asked if he knew anyone named Angel because he felt he needed to pray for her. His friend did not recognize anyone by that name but suggested that Paul pray for a godly lady in the choir of a local Baptist church. This Lady had recently been diagnosed with throat cancer. Her life as well as her ministry and career as a gospel singer were in jeopardy. After his friend introduced them, Paul spent some time building her faith with praises of God and his miraculous works. When asked to pray, Paul was led by the Holy Spirit to be careful to operate in the faith she had as a Baptist church member, within the teachings she had been indoctrinated with. He left with peace that he had accomplished the task as God intended. He inquired about her health several weeks later and was told she'd gotten worse. She continued to go downhill until the time of her surgery. After performing the pre-surgical testing phase of her cancer removal, the surgeon informed her that surgery would not be needed, the cancer was gone! God had performed a wondrous miracle and healed her. This did not take Paul by surprise for he knew God had arranged their meeting and would confirm his word with signs following.

The Lord Is Asking For Thee

Paul began to hear the voice of his grandfather preaching within his spirit night and day. He earnestly looked forward to sleep in order to see his grandfather preaching incredibly wonderful sermons in his dreams. These sermons would echo within him during waking and sleeping hours. Paul prayed to the Father, for him to be given the gift of preaching in a similar manner and the answer changed his life, as well as the lives of others he would influence from then on.

The desire to preach became a reality in his heart as his lips uttered this blessed thought. Paul "The Preacher" began preaching the word of God everywhere he went.

Psalms 37:4

"Delight thyself also in the LORD: and He shall give thee the desires of thine heart."

Paul can still recall the way God answered his prayer and how the call to preach the gospel of Jesus Christ was revealed to him. He had just entered one of these beautiful dreams listening to his grandfather preach and telling God that he would not mind preaching if he could preach like his grandfather when without warning, the reflections of preaching stopped within him. He heard the voice of God say, "Fear not Paul! For I AM The LORD thy God! The God of thy grandfather, The God of Abraham, of Isaac, and of Jacob; I am calling you to prophesy in My Name, and to teach people to have faith.

Be not concerned with their faces (people's acceptance) for I am with thee to deliver thee and to show myself strong with thee, Paul." This voice spoke with authority and Paul sensed a surge of Electricity charge his whole body and fill the room he was in.

Jeremiah 1:4-9
"Then the word of the LORD came unto me, saying, Before I formed thee in the belly I knew thee; and before thou camest forth out of the womb I sanctified thee, and I ordained thee a prophet untothe nations."

The Class Room

After the "Angel" incident took place, the relationship between the lady and Paul's friend's church family increased. They planned to join with several other area churches to attend a Christian retreat in the hopes of growing in their relationships and discipleship with Christ. They made two different trips to this retreat and Paul was able to join them. During the first trip, Paul was on medical leave from work due to hernia surgery and the Lord persuaded him to go. A pastor friend Mr. X and a preaching partner, The Intimidator, went also. Mr. X had met Paul when he was a teenager in a local gang and had befriended him in hopes of leading him to a better life style. Mr. X and the Intimidator rode in the car but the group convinced Paul to ride with them in the bus. During the trip, a few of the riders on the bus expressed disbelief of the "Angel's" healing and other The Preachers friend had witnessed and discussed with them. Ironically, one of the unbelievers was a Deacon who operated the soundboard for the church the healed singer attended. Paul was harassed on the trip with remarks like, "Why don't you prophecy prophet?" or "Why don't you ask God to tell you about...." (Specific persons in the group).

Paul responded, "Folks, I can't turn this gift on or off. It's God! He does what He wants when He wants, and sometimes He chooses to use me when He decides to act. I haven't heard G... " The Preacher paused in speaking because The Holy Spirit had just moved in him. He had not turned around to see who was in the seat behind him but spoke with authority, "...but as for the guy behind me, God just told me that he is going to excel in this retreat." The crowd mocked him in disbelief and the boldness of God swelled in The Preacher and he replied, "Thus saith The Holy Ghost: not only are you going to excel, but you're going to bust a gasket as well!"

The deacon's email address was "Excel", which Paul had no way of knowing.

Their class was called to a halt one day due to a sound outside the premises like that of a bay hound wailing for several minutes. Paul checked to see where "Excel" was but his seat was empty. He was the one in the corridor, "busting a gasket", on fire for the Lord! After the retreat, he returned to his church and would not let anyone near the sound booth unless they were strong Christians and had prayed before approaching the booth. On the last day of the retreat "Excel" announced to several hundred people that when he first met The Preacher he thought that he was crazy... and still did, but knew he was a man of God. Another event at the retreat occurred when it was time to pray over the sign-in ledger for all the attendees. The overseers of the camp had two people praying over the ledger twenty-four hours a day. When it was Paul's allotted time to pray, his partner was The Intimidator. (Mr.X had attended as on observer only). The elders of the camp listened to the prayers in secret. The Intimidator and Paul did not know the people attending the retreat, but they read each name and prayed as the Lord lead them. They took turns reading the names and would ask each other of God's leading for that individual before they prayed. This would have been very embarrassing, even impossible to do if they had known they were being monitored. God manifested Himself in discerning the very needs and hearts of the people. We may only be aware of a name, but God knows every secret thing. In all the years they had participated in the retreat, the elders had never seen God reveal himself in such a strong way. The elders approached The Intimidator to see if Paul would consider preaching for them at the retreat. The Intimidator responded that all that was needed was to place a Bible near Paul when the Spirit of God was present.

Paul was a team leader assigned to a small group with specific projects to complete. On the first project, the elders decided to test his group and give them a failing grade for their effort. Paul was upset and was determined not to fail again.

The next project for his group was to act out a part of the Bible. The LORD gave Paul the Pearl of Great Price parable. The group took great effort in bringing out the details of the story of a man walking along a field one day and found a hidden treasure that did not belong to him. The trespasser asked the owner to sell the land and even though the price was high, the prize was greater. He was willing to spend every penny he had, including his earthly inheritance, in order to buy the field. He sold the greater portion of his positions in society, trying to get the owner to decrease the price, but the owner stood firm. The man finally succumbed and sold all he had to buy the field, determined to have the prize of the treasure. While admiring his newly bought property, a friend came along bemoaning the man's purchase, saying, "I can't believe that you have bought this ugly piece of ground. I surely cannot believe that you have given up your house, your inheritance, and everything else you own to obtain this!" The man replied, "Friend, you don't understand. I have found a great treasure hidden on this land." The friend replied, "That doesn't belong to you, it belongs to the man who sold you the land." The new owner argued that the deed plainly stated that all things on and in the field were now his. Paul played the part of the new owner in the skit and when he reached for the costume jewelry representing the treasure, the elders had replaced it with his Bible. When Paul touched that bible, the preacher in him manifested, rose up and he preached to the retreat, with such enthusiasm that he even hung from the rafters.

Paul's friend, The Intimidator, was standing up in a chair jumping up and down with excitement as the spirit of God descended upon all that were in the room. (Remember Paul had just undergone hernia surgery. This was physically impossible! It was the manifestation of God's power and gifts, which left him with no pain and no damage to his stitches.) The elders went out of the building to discuss this event and soon returned with their grade for Paul's project.

They came in and turned the lights off for this event was held at night. The leader of the elders shinned his flashlight on the floor to where the buried treasure was supposed to be and started preaching under the Lord's anointing. God was again allowing the Holy Spirit to descend upon those in the room with power. All in the room was in total awe and worshiped as the Living God took charge of the service and Paul's group received an A+ for their project.

Matthew 13:44-46

"Again, the kingdom of heaven is like unto treasure hid in field; the which when a man hath found, he hide, and for joy thereof goeth and selleth all that he hath, and buyeth that field".

{Author's note: I have found recorded in church history over the years, in the great revivals of years gone by, all of the works of the Holy Spirit were in operation in one way or another}

The Journey Begins
(The Methodist Years)

The "call" came soon after Paul's salvation. Paul asked the elders of his denomination the meaning of prophesy. They told him, "Don't worry about that, all of that has long since passed away with the founding fathers of the faith. Whatever you've been hearing must be of the devil." Paul continued to be instructed by God on the gift of prophecy. Because of their instructions, Paul settled for renewing the promise that he had made to GOD as a child. This went on for three years as Pastor Faith and his partner Pastor Hope poured "The WORD" into Paul and the call to preach was realized. However, the call to prophecy was suppressed by the doctrine of the organization. The voice of God continued as Paul submitted himself to His Word, and resisted the temptations offered by this wicked and cruel world.
James 4:7

"Submit yourselves therefore to God. Resist the devil, and he will flee from you."

Paul felt the call to preach at a small church in Tennessee and did not venture farther out for a long time. Eventually, visiting preachers would ask him to preach on their radio programs. The first time his mother heard him on the radio, she ran around the house shouting and rejoicing over her once wayward Son, now serving God. On a visitation to a man's home, Paul was instructed by the Holy Spirit to bring the anointing oil from the car because a devil was present inside the house.

Neither Pastor Faith nor Paul had any experience in casting out demons but the mercy of God, in the form of the Holy Spirit, spoke so they could minister effectively on that call. The gentleman requested prayer soon after being introduced; stating that he thought there was an evil spirit tormenting him.

Pastor Faith and Paul were able to cast out the evil spirit with the Word of knowledge from God and the anointing with oil. He was later told that the oil represents the presence of the LORD and His blood. Affirmation of this came when a fellow truck driver called The Messenger (on the CB Radio) related an incident to Paul concerning a lady who asked a pastor to anoint her house with oil to cast off the spell of a wizard (a male witch) who was harassing her. The wizard visited her and asked why her house was covered with blood and left, never to return. As The Preacher began to develop into the plan of God, he remembers seeing the physical manifestation of Angels. Paul remembers one worship service that impacted his life and ministry. While he was preaching, several people were at the front of the church, worshipping at the altar, and Paul noticed a woman in the back of the church smiling broadly at him. She stood up and entered a Sunday school room. This particular room was always locked and was not in use. Paul asked everyone present who the lady was and no one could answer him. None of the others had seen her! Paul began having similar supernatural occurrences but he kept most of them to himself. He would preach as often as he could. He was blessed to witness people being saved, as the power of the Holy Spirit would rain down on them. Having been indoctrinated in the Methodist church, Paul was unaware there was more to faith than what he had been exposed to.

Paul completed as many seminary correspondence courses as he could. He received several certificates of completion.

During this time period he was invited to a Bible College in Kentucky and was allowed to live in a dorm for a few weeks with a friend named, Encouragement, who was a student there. The facility of this school gave Paul this opportunity and allowed him to attend classes with his friend that he might see what campus life was all about. They also wanted to give Paul a chance to see if he would like to enroll in their school.

It did not take Paul long to become very disappointed in the activities of the other students. They lounged around the dorm rooms in their underwear and drank alcohol while writing or even copying someone else's sermons for class. Paul felt the strong presence of the LORD to reprove, rebuke, and exhort the other students. A few of them repented and several spoke up in class, testifying about their behavior, to the point of being expelled. The other students did not repent, however, and there were three unexplained deaths at the school within the week. These deaths brought reverential fear into the school's community and the student's attitudes changed.

11Timothy 4:2

"Preach the word; be instant in season, out of season; reprove, rebuke, exhort with all longsuffering and doctrine."

On a more positive note, Paul's friend Encouragement was a unique preacher at school who was also from Somewhere, Tennessee. They had become good friends before school. Encouragement had joined a Holiness church and invited Paul to come also. They would visit from time to time, attending the small church his friend had joined. While praying for Paul during a service, his friend laid hands on him. He asked the LORD to baptize him with the Holy Spirit and to give him the evidence of speaking in tongues.

Paul had been taught that the Holy Spirit baptized him when he was saved, which differed from his friend's beliefs. His friend agreed that he had gotten the Holy Spirit when he was saved but told him that now he needed the Holy Spirit to get him!

Revelation 22:17

"And the Spirit and the bride say, come. And let him that heareth say, Come. And let him that is athirst come. And whosoever will, let him take the water of life freely."

Paul had been preaching against this type of nonsense for over three years. He would say that Holiness people were "like a bunch of geese going after the same ear of corn." His grandfather had often commented on the quality of singing during Holiness services, but felt they did not have any order to their services. He told Paul that God always works in order; therefore the Holiness movement could not be of God. His Grandfather was right, yet at the same time he was wrong. Pauls' first experience with this type of doctrine was during a camping trip his grandfather had taken him on with Native American Indians. The Indians were near the river worshipping God and he decided to join them. They had loaned him an electric guitar to play during the worship service. The women in the congregation began to twitch, jerk, and were falling from their chairs. He ran back to his grandfather's campsite in fear. He later learned that his grandfather was correct in the godly order instructions but was wrong about the Holiness movement. Shortly after his friend had prayed for him, he began speaking beautiful languages he did not know or understand. He was afraid that he was blaspheming God so he did not exercise his gift and quenched the Spirit. God showed Paul a present in a dream. It was half open and had green ribbons around it.

Paul asked what the present was and God told him it was a gift from God that he had only half opened but Paul didn't understand and asked God to explain about this new gift.

The Spirit of God told him the gift of baptism was only half opened and he quickly told God that he wanted it all and everything that went with the gift. The beautiful languages returned to him immediately and brought a charge of electricity within him each time he used it. He decided to keep this information to himself out of fear that the organizations he belonged to would not understand.

His friend also gave Paul a book by Brother Kenneth Hagin that addressed the gift of hearing from God. It was not long before Paul experienced the manifestation of this wonderful Spirit revealing to him of its presence and power. Later, Paul purchased all the books he could find from this author who seemed to know what he was talking about. Paul felt privileged when asked to preach to the young boys and girls at a Bible Camp. Their simple faith manifested was more delightful to him than words can express. He attended evangelistic meetings at a girl's camp. He saw great results achieved in the kingdom with many conversions of young people. He was mowing the grass at home when he felt an overwhelming desire to preach to the boy's camp the following week. He prayed for the opportunity and noticed his father waving to him as soon as the prayer was finished. He was called to the phone to speak to the director of the camp who asked him if he was willing to preach to the boys the next week! The LORD blessed the service and thirteen boys came forward during the altar call for salvation that night. The Spirit moved on another boy who informed Paul the next day that he had received Christ at bedtime that previous night. The congregation of his home church voted Paul in as an associate pastor.

He remembers an incident with the church's neighbor after finding a note taped on the front door. There was an enormous apple tree, abundant with apples, growing along the fence line between the two properties. The tree overshadowed more of the church's property than the neighbor's. The note demanded that the children of the church were to stop eating the apples on either side of the fence, stating that the apples were the sole property of the neighbor. Although this angered the congregation of the church, they held prayer for the property owner's attitude. They instructed everyone to refrain from eating any of the apples.

In less than a week, the wind from a sudden storm uprooted the apple tree without harming a utility building the root system was growing underneath! The tree landed on the church property in front of the door where the note had been left.

God had left His answer to the note in an awesome demonstration of His power. The neighbor's response was to quickly move.

Genesis 12:3

"And I will bless them that bless thee, and curse him that curseth thee..."

In the latter years of his associate pastor-ship, Paul was employed in Somewhere, TN. He was hired as a first class diesel mechanic with a national trucking company he had informed the management of his ministry before being hired. Paul was trained to be an exceptional mechanic and continually was found witnessing to fellow employees including people in management positions. His witnessing was hindered, but not quenched, because of the performance of his work.

John 3:19-21

"And this is the condemnation, that light is come into the world, and men loved darkness rather than light, because their deeds were evil."

One particular manager may have liked Paul, but joked with him in a horrible way. He would call Paul into his office and tell him he was fired. He would allow him to walk out, then call him back again to say he was kidding and for him to return to work. Paul felt tormented daily. This manager verbally ridiculed his call as a preacher, played practical jokes on him, and one day went too far.

He drugged Paul's coffee and personally handed him the drink. He then bragged to the other managers and they were all laughing at Paul. In an attempt to be funny, one of the company's dispatchers asked Paul the next day where his dope was, Paul replied, "It's out in the car. It's called King James!" Then Paul handed him a gospel tract. The front of the tract read: DON'T GET CAUGHT and opened to DEAD, WITH OUT JESUS! ... It also had a picture of a coffin on the opposing page. The dispatcher turned pale and never mocked Paul again.

II Timothy 3:12

"Yea and all that will live godly in Christ Jesus shall suffer persecution".

The same week Paul was drugged, his manager's brother, was beaten and shot to death and his father was hospitalized with an unknown ailment. He then asked Paul to pray for his father to recover. Paul answered him, "You'd know better than to drug the man of God!"

He did not think he was wrong in drugging Paul and did not repent. His father died the next day. The next Monday the company went bankrupt. Thirty-five mechanics and many others lost their jobs in one building alone. The building Paul worked in has never had a successful business to occupy it again, although many have tried. This building and property remains a deteriorating structure to this day.

Psalms 105:15

"Saying, Touch not mine anointed, and do my prophets no harm."

Paul had purchased a nearly new vehicle to make the one hundred and twenty mile round trip to and from this job. When the company closed, he was unable to make his car payments.

The LORD told him to do something he thought was very unusual. He told him to walk around his car seven times, praying as he went. He later felt this was an exercise in helping his faith overcome the overwhelming wall of difficulty in his life. To Paul's amazement, people who had borrowed money from him in the past started paying him. They would call, stop by, or mail him money. God's provision was proven. The greatest event to happen out of these circumstances occurred eighteen years later. Paul had just passed an eighteen wheeler dump truck on a Kentucky highway and noticed that the driver was a black man. Paul picked up his CB mike and politely thanked the driver for flashing his headlights signaling to him that he could come back over in his lane. The man asked Paul his CB handle (code name) and Paul replied, they call me The Preacher because I am a minister of the gospel to the truckers.

The man replied that his CB handle was wooden leg. This sent chills down Paul's spine as he remembered the black man that he worked with as a mechanic eighteen years earlier in a small shop in Somewhere, Tennessee. Paul picked up the mike and related to the man that he once knew and worked with a man called by that name. The man instantly informed Paul that he remembered him and that his life in front of him had been instrumental in God bringing him into His fold. Wooden Leg, a fellow mechanic that Paul had worked with and witnessed to, was moved by the testimony Paul had lived in front of him. Paul had the great pleasure of meeting him as a newly saved Christian and was informed that he had been instrumental in God's plan. Wooden Leg and his entire family joined a church and were living a happy Christian life. The mental trauma Paul had suffered under this daily persecution and the events of the last week on this job had broken his spirit. He no longer cared for himself. His focus turned and was driven even more to ministry and caring for others than it had ever been before. This "over" caring is what ended this period of ministry in Pau's' life.

The Backslidden Condition

(Seven long years)

Paul's mental state deteriorated from the heavy burden of stress and he had a psychological breakdown. He had married before he was saved and the problems involved in a Christian/Non- Christian marriage contributed to his fragile mental state. He had been warned in a dream to investigate this woman before marrying her but he ignored the warning and paid the price. His parents were advised by his physician to institutionalize him for treatment. Eventually, this forced him to become a coast-to-coast truck driver in order to protect his individual rights. He knew he had to get away from the stresses that were bringing him to the breaking point, he became a recluse. He began to hate everything and everyone, preachers in particular. Paul immersed himself in the trucking industry to help ease his suffering. Before Paul went trucking, his church organization curtailed his true call to Prophecy and suppressed the gift of tongues. The end result was a volcano of Spiritual release boiling inside his soul. He worked as a mechanic for other pastors, who would often pay too little or not at all for his services. This added to his opinion of disgust for others in the ministry. Due to his rapidly diminishing finances, he worked three jobs; a mechanic by day, security guard by night and as a part-time deputy. He was also preaching in churches and on radio broadcasts as God permitted. He allowed very little rest for his mind & body. God however, took this opportunity to educate him further with His Word. The security job, in particular, allowed him time to study the Bible and speak to His Spirit. This was the highlight of his day, page after page of study as the Voice of God instructed him in His Word.

John 14:26

"But the Comforter, which is the Holy Ghost, whom the Father will send in my name, He shall teach you all things, and bring all things to your remembrance."

Paul was under persecution from the overseer's council because of the unusual manifestations observed when he preached. His senior pastor, Brother Faith, always supported him when approached by the council. Paul was finally called in to answer to the elders of the organization regarding attending services outside the organization. Paul affirmed their accusations and did not try to hide anything from them. He was not aware he was breaking organizational rules by attending other churches. Despite his ignorance of the rules, he was asked to resign and did so. Paul then asked this district overseer if he could preach in his church and an appointment was made. When the service ended, the overseer announced to his congregation that, against his wishes, the organization would pull Paul's license to preach. He also stated that he could find no fault with Paul. Shortly before the inquisition, Paul's grandfather had resigned from this organization and went independent. Paul was convinced this was a part of what led to him being brought before the elders. He continued preaching under Pastor Faith for a year and a half before affiliating himself with another organization. He found, to his regret, more rejection toward the gifts that were operating in his ministry. This led to more frustration and countless wrong thoughts about carnal preachers. For the remainder of these early ministry years, Paul became an independent preacher. He was blessed with as many and sometimes more appointments to preach than he had before. When God closes a door he always opens another. Through his part-time work at the sheriff's department, Paul became involved with several individuals with demented personalities.

Some knew him because they had heard him preach on the radio. Paul would try to help them but saw little progress made. They would call him during his off duty hours and he would always respond. He believes the one thing he learned during this time was that a man needs to rest. He was always on call for anyone and hadn't learn this lesson in time. In another incident, a fellow officer's son had cut his eye and the officer's wife called Paul at home asking for prayer. She was a woman of faith and had heard of his healing ministry. He told her to place her hand on her son's eye and agree with him in prayer. She removed her hand after praying and the eye was totally healed with no scar or any sign of damage left. The Lord was showing himself strong in the man that he had personally trained by his spirit to be a leader in the end time revival that would be an all out effort of the Kingdom of God to rescue as many as possible from the enemy.

In another incident, Paul was helping the altar ministry at a friend's church when a lady came to church wearing an oversized shoe to hide her burnt foot. Paul usually doesn't make it his business to notice what people are wearing or how they looked when he is in a service because he is more concerned with what God has planned and does not want to miss out on his will. When the pastor prayed for the woman, she was slain in the spirit and was caught by the catchers who would make sure she was decent and undisturbed. The Spirit compelled Paul to lean down and pray for her ankle and he did so without drawing attention to what he was doing. Later in the service the pastor asked Paul for a song. Paul started to sing the hymn when he was prompted by the Spirit to inquire what was wrong with the lady's foot. She had been ashamed and did not want anyone to know about it. She suddenly screamed in excitement because the foot, swollen from injury, was shrinking in her shoe at that very moment! This caused Paul to realize that the gift of the Word of Knowledge was starting to work in his ministry.

Two Episodes of Angels

Hebrews 13:2

"Be not forgetful to entertain strangers: for thereby some have entertained angels unawares."

Paul remembers the very moment he passed a line and no longer wanted anything to do with church or people altogether. He felt an electrical shock snap inside his brain and knew he had gone too far. He made the decision to step out of the ministry and seek worldly employment and entertainment. He then decided to drive coast-to-coast. He heard the Voice of God say, "Son, I know deep down in your heart you still love me!" Paul did not even bother to reply. He began to conform to the lifestyle of the worldly and changed his appearance to match. He let his hair grow out and had it perm so that he might blend in with the crowd. He noticed a very attractive lady at a dancing club one night and walked by her table. She invited him to sit and he eagerly accepted. He had noticed other women in the room seemed to be flirting with him. The waitresses were also and he had known them for a long time. He wondered what was going on as he made small talk with the pretty lady. She asked if he wanted to taste her drink and he did. He spit it out on the floor and exclaimed, "That's water!" She replied, "It sure is! And man of God, I have been sent here to warn you! You had better get your act together!" At that moment, the Spirit of God ran through him with a tremendous force and threw him out of his chair onto the floor. Paul scurried to his feet and left quickly. He and wanted to get home as fast as he could. The next day his aunt called to discuss a dream she had the night before. She could sense that the forces of darkness were after his very life. Paul did not care at this point and did not turn back to God. He began a losing battle with his nerves, ignoring his call to ministry and himself.

The Preacher did not want to rest or take any time from his work as he tried to maintain what little mental competence he had left. He was sitting in a truck stop thinking of the sin he had committed the night before and thinking he had now blown any chance to be a minister of the gospel. A tall elderly white man, in a torn sweater, held the door for him as they were leaving the Georgia truck stop. The man said, "I need to talk to you, just because someone falls back into the world, or has messed up with the opposite flesh, it's not the end of the world. God sent me to you!" That captured Paul's attention!

The man continued, "You have a great testimony and can help a lot of people. You have a history of being involved with the wrong crowds and still have a bad reputation for the life you have lived in front of them." Then the glory of God filled his eyes as he said, "God can use you." He reminded Paul about his teenage years and the fact that God had delivered him from the gang lifestyle he was living. The messenger continued, "God has a plan for your life!

You have read: "*For that which I do I allow not: for what I would, that do I not; but what I hate, that do I. If then I do that which I would not, I consent unto the law that it is good. Now then it is no more I that do it, but sin that dwelleth in me. For I know that in me (that is, in my flesh,) dwelleth no good thing: for to will is present with me: but how to perform that which is good I find not. For the good that I would I do not: but the evil, which I would not, that I do. Now if I do that I would not, it is no more I that do it, but sin that dwelleth in me. I find then a law, that, when I would do good, evil is present with me. For I delight in the law of God after the inward man. But I see another law in my members, warring against the law of my mind, and bringing me into captivity to the law of sin, which is in my members.*

Oh wretched man that I am! Who shall deliver me from the body of this death? I thank God through Jesus Christ our Lord. So then with the mind I myself serve the law of God; but with the flesh the law of sin".(Romans 7:15-25)

"One day your past will help countless others. You're not ready for it now, but you will be later. You have never imagined how beautiful heaven is, and I know that you are going to make it."

Paul turned to wave to a fellow truck driver and when he turned back to continue the conversation, the gentleman was gone. Many years later, Paul was leading another trucker to Christ in a Wyoming restaurant when he saw this same man at the driver's counter, smiling at him benevolently.

When he turned his head, the man was gone again. One morning, after nearly four years of running virtually non-stop, northeast to southwest, coast to coast, Paul stopped at a Truck Stop in Somewhere, TX. He had participated in plenty of illegal activities there in the past so he was very familiar with this particular area. It was a Sunday morning and Chaplain Wonderful tried to witness to him in the truck stop. Paul pulled a sharp knife and told him he would cut his throat. He yelled, "Get away from me! I don't like preachers! I've seen them running out of women's houses, acting still as if they were goody goodies, doing all sorts of underhanded things behind people's backs. I have already tried that lifestyle, and I don't want it!" Chaplain Wonderful sadly left him alone. Later that morning, while in the shower, The Voice spoke to Paul and said, "You pulled your knife on one of mine. I want you to go to that Chapel this morning. I need you to go, Paul!" He couldn't find it in his heart to turn God's Voice down.

He had learned to hate the ways of so-called preachers but could not hate the tender love of The Voice he knew so well. Paul went to the small trucker's chapel that morning. The LORD had a guitar waiting for him once again.

He played both before and after the service. He talked with the small crowd and explained how God had used his grandfather to teach him many of the old hymns. He remembered his papaw picking a banjo and squirrels would sit on his shoulders, appearing to listen to the melodies he played. Paul finally broke down and testified, "I've just come through a lot. I love God! But, I've just come through so much. My nerves are shot. I haven't been living it. I'm not going to stand here, and pretend like something I'm not!" Even though, as a small boy, he did not understand the meaning behind the songs his grandfather sang, he could feel his passion and the same sincerity began flowing through his heart in testimony to God's glory. Paul sang, "Sinner, hear me when I say, Fall down on your knees and pray! I'd rather be in a deep dark grave, and to know that my soul was saved, than to live in this world in a house of gold, and deny my God and lose my soul!" Paul elaborated on his grandfather's ministry, his life, and walk with Jesus.

The altar call was given and an entire family came forward to trust Jesus as their LORD and Savoir. Paul, had trouble understanding how God could still use him, or how he could even love him in this backslidden condition. Sometime later, Chaplain Wonderful called him and said, "Paul, you know something, when you were in the chapel that morning, giving your testimony and singing, do you remember the family that came forward? That same family had been coming to the chapel for over a year.

I had preached my heart out and never could get them to move. Paul, with the anointing of the Spirit, it was your honesty that morning that compelled them to come forward and give their hearts and lives to Jesus!" Paul replied, "That he did remember the event and hoped he never forgot it! Wonderful said "Paul they all were killed the following week, in a plane crash, the whole family. This shook Paul to the core. Paul knew that he was living in a nightmare and was unable to change without help.

He began to call for help from the bottom of his soul. The Preacher was in California, around a month later, and had a disquieting dream. He saw a cancerous leg, ready to fall off, a body and his grandfather was also in the dream. In the dream, Paul asked him the meaning behind the vision, and his grandfather told him it was his nerves. He returned to Tennessee to see his grandfather for reassurance. His grandfather said, "You have troubled me: TROUBLED ME, I SAY! Let's go to the barn." The barn was his favorite place to pray and while there, he told Paul he had dreamed the same vision. He prayed and praised God from one end of the barn to the other; covering the straw rich ground with holy tears for his grandson.

Paul knew he was special to his grandfather, because he was the only other preacher in the family. He testified to Paul of his own conversion experience. He initially told God that he had other plans for his life, and refused the call. God gave him a dream of the "death angel" departing heaven's Glory to come for his soul. He decided that he had better obey the LORD. Another friend of Paul's had also delayed his call for too long. He was driven more into prayer when his youngest son was born with polio and was told he would never be able to walk.

(This son became an incredible vocalist in his adult years), Paul did not know if this disobedience to God's call was a factor, but it weighed heavily on his mind, and reminded him that he too was pushing God's mercy and grace to the limit. Paul knew that His love toward him was unconditional, but God's judgment is inevitable. God does have a cutting off time (a matter of the heart). He wanted Paul to learn what His mercy was all about. Paul had heard both ministers and non-ministers, preaching and teaching with a closed fist, showing no mercy to others. They would ridicule others from the pulpit, trying to force the outside to clean up, instead of allowing God to sanctify them for holy living, from the inside.

They preached out of hurt, not love, and Paul had been just like them in the past. A man in his congregation had recently moved away from his wife and children, to live with another woman. Paul had not been scheduled to preach, yet found himself in the pulpit, when the man was in attendance. Paul, preached in righteous indignation instead of ministering with God's Holy Spirit, He had visited the deserted family earlier and witnessed their poverty. He used the pulpit to further his indignation stating, "That the man would tear a hole in his pocket before giving his children a dime"! Paul's father tried to warn him that he would regret the sermons preached in anger, hurting, and ridiculing others, because they were different. Paul The Preacher later admitted to his father that he had been wrong in preaching hurt instead of love.

{*Author's note: In this novel, God allowed The Preacher to find out what Mercy really is and what Grace is! He showed Paul that we do not deserve any of it. It is only by His divine will that we can ever receive it.*}

Along the same time line that Paul met the first Angel in the honky-tonk; his hairstylist began flirting with him. She tried to get him to date her girlfriends when he turned her down. His bad marriage left him distrustful of women and he wasn't interested in dating anyone at the time. She asked him to let her read his palm to tell his fortune. Paul was aware that this was an abomination, to God, but at the time, he didn't really care, one way or another. She told him he would be a short, then long haul truck driver, and suddenly looked at him in fear. She jerked her hands back and insisted that he leave immediately. She would not cut his hair or take his phone calls any more. Her friends also avoided him from that time on. Paul still has no idea what happened that caused this woman to run from him or what this woman was allowed to see.

Day Dreaming Into Reality

(The Third Angel)

Paul worked hard at staying on the road and his spiritual condition was deteriorating steadily. He would try to serve God in faith and his wife would be unfaithful to him. On a run through Ohio, he held his fingers to heaven and told God he was hanging by a thread. Proceeding to the security guard's office at his loading destination, he told the security guard, "If these lumpers lie or jerk me around, don't bother just calling the law: call the coroner, too. I am in no mood to be messed with!" Paul was relieved when all went well. Part of his frustration involved a financial deal he had become involved in and realized was a terrible mistake. He was in the process of making a deal with investors, in Missouri, to build the truck stop of his dreams. They drew up plans to build a western style truck stop, in a horseshoe shape, with plate glass windows, ten feet in the middle, running to eight feet on the ends. Hanging plants, graphic lighting, and every amenity a truck driver would ever need, including movie theaters, barber shops, etc... and the plans were for Paul to manage the facility. He had always loved western wear and had been influenced by his paternal grandfather, nicknamed Cowboy. He was born, in Wyoming, but he later moved to share a farm in Tennessee with Paul's father. His father bragged on Cowboy's marksmanship and told Paul he saw him shoot a crow out of the sky with a Colt 44 pistol. He permanently injured his leg in a rodeo competition and was forced to retire. Paul inherited his talent with guns. He also had an outlaw relative named Kenny Sure Shot who could shoot five marbles in the air with a .38 pistol. As you have guessed, the western theme naturally appealed to Paul but he became disillusioned with the contractor's morals and cancelled the deal. Paul drove to the Petro truck stop in Girard, OH.

His thoughts were focused on the love he felt while serving God, in particular, making lighted crosses for other trucker's rigs. The man seemed to come out of nowhere and approached Paul in a way as if he had met him before. He was a thin, young, black man and had a confident smile on his face. Paul was raised in the heart of bigotry and prejudice in the south. The trucking companies he worked for had always sent him on the "big" city runs. At that time, black men were employed to lump (load and unload) trucks. There were several incidents involving Paul and the lumpers fighting and being arrested or being permanently barred from the premises.

God had to change his attitude on prejudices. He was feeling sorry for himself, thinking he had lost any future he ever had. They sat in the back booth of a restaurant and waited for their coffee to be served. Paul was grieving inside over the continual unfaithfulness of his spouse, whom he dearly loved. He thought of the letters he had written declaring this love for her. He had taught her to drive big rigs in an effort to draw them closer to each other. It had the opposite effect and her trucking career was quickly over. The thin young man snapped Paul out of his stupor by saying, "Preacher! God sent me to you!"

Paul was dressed to look like a country singer with western style clothing, long perm hair, cowboy boots, and a black Stetson hat. He asked the young man if he looked like a preacher to him. Determined to continue, the man replied, "Oh, preacher don't get mad. God sent me to tell you to stop straddling the fence. Now, don't feel bad 'cause God has a lot of pastors and preachers who are straddling the fence." He placed the salt and peppershaker side-by-side, pointed to them and said, "If you'll get off on one side or the other, He can deal with you. But you're straddling the fence and you need to get off on one side or the other! He proclaimed that God does not ordain all marriages.

Sometimes we go get one (spouse) on our own. God does not expect you to put up with all that you have been putting up with." Paul quickly rebutted, "I love my wife, thank-you! She's just got a problem. She likes other men. She's got a weakness, and I'm trying to help her through it." The messenger sternly repeated, "God sent me to tell you that He does not sanction all marriages. Let me tell you how to handle all that is to come against you and you will know what to do when it comes to pass." Paul rudely ignored the messenger and called his wife from the table. She immediately announced that she was not happy and had decided she could not handle their marriage any longer. Humbled by her once again, he said, "Well... ok" and hung up the phone. Paul gave the messenger a lighted cross that he had made. The man strongly suggested that Paul give it to another driver but Paul sensing in his spirit that this may be an Angel of God insisted that he take it and the man did just that. One event before Paul went trucking was when he began working as a diesel mechanic in Alabama. The chaplain for the Alabama State Highway Patrol would often visit his work site to talk with the drivers. He persuaded Paul to attend a service at his home church.

Paul was unsure if God was still interested in using him in ministry and prayed for a sign from God at the service. That evening, the Chaplain preached his life spelled out under the anointing of the LORD God Almighty. Paul found the way to Godly repentance and felt himself going down to the altar with prayers of earnest tears and a contrite heart. After this anointing, every step towards God and the ministry would result in devastation in his personal life. His life style was unacceptable to a called man of God and he began to realize it. Paul tried to convince his ex-wife to change her lifestyle and told her he was finished with the bar scene.

She chose to remain the way she was and he told her she would regret not turning to God.

Paul's life was overwhelmed with disappointment. He fought against the inclination to take his own life. He was miserable from all the mistakes he had made in his life and Satan fed him the lie that suicide was his only recourse. Satan is an expert at lying to God's people and tormenting them with their past. Paul cannot remember the details of his first attempt and only remembers he was interrupted and changed his mind. His second attempt was at Grandma's Truck Stop on I-65 in Indiana. a goodbye message for his family on the company's personal voice mail. He heard a horrible sound when he picked up a phone in the restaurant and this happed on two more phones. He rudely asked the waitress if they had any phones that worked in the place. She led him to a working phone and a friend of Paul's (he had not seen in years) was sitting nearby. His friend said, "I know what you're going to try to do. I've heard about you. You don't want to do it. You don't want to do what you're thinking about! That's why you've met me here today." The shock of this declaration changed his mind again. The third attempt occurred at the All American Truck Stop in Carlisle, PA. Paul was determined this time. He stepped out of the truck with a pistol in his hand. He went up the cat-walk (the walk platform on the back of trucks) and readied the weapon to fire. He had placed the muzzle of the gun under his chin and began squeezing the trigger. Someone suddenly began yelling at him and turned his attention toward the trucker's chapel and Paul felt an irresistible need to be there! Paul met Chaplain Love and his wife Mercy there. Chaplain Love had retired from the Navy and Mercy was a tiny fireball of a redhead. They both had traveled all over the nation, winning drivers to the LORD. Most of the chapels were mobile in the early years.

Paul told them his story. Chaplain Love cried and his wife Mercy ministered to Paul out of the Word of God. She pointed him to the scriptures directly related to his situation.

She and Chaplain Love prayed with Paul. For the next several years, Paul would stop in to visit whenever he was nearby. The LORD was working to return him to ministry. Paul testifies to God's Word that He knows us from before the foundation of the world. He has every hair on our heads counted. Not even one hair falls out without Him realizing it. He knows our near future and distant end in Heaven. Paul was unable to understand how God would accomplish the entire ministry in him because it was well beyond him and even his current existence. He feels wonder at the way God knows him now, knew him in the past, and had seen his future. God has already seen him in heaven. Paul The Preacher explains, "I do not know how he is going to accomplish this task of His love. It is beyond my imagination, beyond my expansion of my mind, to understand just how He is going to bring me out of this dark trial that I have been going through. I know that He will bring me out. He did not anoint me so highly to leave me. He will not leave you or me nor forsake us. He has already seen you make it as well!

{Author's Note: What the world would give to have the assured knowledge of the future. What confidence and boldness would address their each and every day?}

The Tares Appeared

Matthew 13: 25&26

"But while men slept, his enemy came and sowed tares among the wheat, and went his way. But when the blade was sprung up, and brought forth fruit, then appeared the tares also."

I later met The Preacher as he was, in a downcast mood. He was at the same facility that I was and we were both waiting for our load to be loaded. He did not notice my truck parked in the rear of the lot. He had decided to hook up his travel guitar and get in some practice while he was waiting. This particular time, he had decided to hook it up to a small amplifier that he carried with him. I awoke to hear gospel music being played on a guitar. The Preacher is an exceptional musician. I proceeded to walk over and check this out for myself. Could this be my friend or was I dreaming? He was so hurt that he never even noticed when I approached him. Knowing how the Lord had used him to help me caused me to ask him a stern question. I asked in a voice of concern, "have you thanked the Lord in this?" I think this shook him up but he tried to ward it off by saying, "you just don't know." I replied, "It doesn't matter because the steps of a good man are ordered by the lord." The Preacher confided in me that it seems as though a person can spend their whole life building something for the lord, and one person can tear it down in one night. He said that people were losing their love and zeal for one another and that even church people acted different once they would depart from a church service. They act like they are in a hurry to worry to get buried. The Preacher said, I know we live in a fast paced world and people are adapted to fast foods and having it their way. They took sixteen years to get into something and want the man of God to fix it in one service.

Everybody wants to be the chief in today's church and they sure do not want to summit to authority. That is why they leave one church and start another one and take the same messed up mind with them. I tell you Little Silas, We need to influence our environment but not let our environment influence or get in us. God is a God of order and authority. If we will not summit to the authority that God has placed over us then it's a sure indication that we will not summit to God. I said, you know Paul, I see where you are going with this and I have to say that it is so true. There is no sacrifice on their part and it's like by passing the cross to get to heaven which is impossible. Paul commented that some churches today are like a sponge which needs to be rung out. He stated that they were always asking and demanding from the congregation and weren't giving anything back. He said that Churches are letting the culture around them go to hell while they are fattening up their own pig. The Preacher went on to say that a lot of people have lost interest in church because of the lack of love and concern. They would rather dress up on a cold day and attend a flea market where at least they know that they are getting something for their dollar. Paul witnessed this first hand as he had done street ministry in rural areas of the big cities for the last 13 years. A lot of his street ministry has been done in the area of prospering well known churches. A person who attended one of these churches once told The Preacher that they had armed guards at this church. The Preacher is well known by the drug gangs, prostitutes, and street people of all races. Other ministers that would attempt to minister in these areas would not be able to survive and their lives would be in danger. God has used the Preacher to clothe, feed and win the trust of these street people in the area would send their children to his truck to ask for bibles.

With a gleam in his eye, The Preacher would comment on how much it blessed him to watch a person hooked on powerful drugs leave his truck with a new blanket, pillow and clothes, walk down the street feeling like Christmas had finally made it to them and that somebody in this world really does care.

I am reminded of a story The Preacher once told me concerning his run in with one of the notorious local gangs in Atlanta, Georgia. He said, Little Silas, "I walked right up to the ring leader and said I will tell you why I do what I do" He said first of all, I have danced with the big boys and not little gangs like you and Almighty God decided to protect me and not throw me away when he had ever reason in the world to do so. He said, Little Silas, "They exclaimed that I was a good man and left me alone. Later, he said this gang came back around where he was and some of the street people warned him to steer clear of them because they were mean to which The Preacher replied that he had already met them. My travels have taken me through some of the areas that The Preacher has ministered in and I have found that the street people have the utmost respect for this man of God. If churches today would grasp the vision of this man of God, they would see a significant change in the atmosphere of their church. The Preacher shared his vision with me and I am going to now attempt to share it with you. Paul said, just as brother Martin Luther King had a dream, I vision seeing those that according to today's church have sinned away their chance of being used in the Lord's work reached and shown a true meaning, purpose and yes the call of Almighty God rekindled in their life. To see the drunk come out from under his makeshift home under a bridge and yes to see a prostitute of a 20 year profession (like Mary in the scriptures) find our Lord and His out stretched hands of Love, lift them up, dust them off and get them the necessary training and materials that will help them be better prepared to go into the enemy's camp and take back what he stole from them.

Yes to see Legion come home and be a new dad and husband to a once tormented wife and children. To see the woman at the well called in to the work of God. To see the withered hand that was drawn up from the lack of circulation, stretched out and restored as whole as the other. The man with the withered hand was in the temple and his hand was useless because of restriction in the blood flow. There are people today with the call of God on their life out in the world because somebody told them that something they did in their past would disqualify them from doing the work God called them to do. My bible tells me in John 1; 9 that IF WE confess our sins that he is faithful to forgive and the Blood of Jesus Christ cleanses us from all sin and unrighteousness. The woman at the well who led a whole city to the Lord would have a hard time getting a job playing the piano in today's church with all of its rules and regulations. I know some preachers who would stand at the door and turn people away from the house of God because of the way they were dressed. Some of these people are lost and searching for answers and we are going to turn them away because of the way they look? Paul looked at me with tears in his eyes and says God help us to realize the value of one soul that will be going out into eternity without God in their life and we were the hindrance that kept them away from the house of God because of the way they were dressed. I asked Paul a question concerning King Solomon and the dedication of the house he built for God. I reminded him that there was a lot of preparation and prayer went in to that work. I also asked the Preacher if he knew what happened to all the thousands of sacrifices that were being made to God on the altars that Solomon had made. I asked, what happened to all that meat? The Preacher got happy and said that is it! I said, 'That is what? He said that the people had a feast. He said that is the answer to today's church problem.

He said, some have already been led by the Spirit to set aside one special day every three months and take out of the church treasury and ask all in the service that are in need of money to come forward and partake of the offering plate that is from the church to them. This would bring the favor and blessing of God on any ministry out reach. He said Little Silas; the King took out of his own pantry and offered thousands of animals for sacrifice for two weeks. There were nearly three million people there partaking of this worship service. Can you imagine being around that many people? He said that it takes two or three days just to get two hundred thousand people into a racing event. What would it be like to be in the presence of a million people gathered in one place? When Solomon dedicated the temple and made an end of praying, God sent fire down from heaven and consumed the burnt offering and the sacrifices till the Glory of God filled the house till the priests could not enter in to minister.

The Levites were training to later become priests, and there was love and unity in the place. The people hungry from their journey consumed the meat and bowed themselves with their faces to the ground upon the pavement and worshipped and praised the Lord, saying; for he is good: for his mercy endureth forever. He said you know something Little Silas, "I miss church." Paul stated that he missed the love, unity, and worship that used to be common place in the old churches. He said, "I miss hearing the old preachers declaring the word of God with a trumpet voice warning people that there is a heaven to gain and a hell to shun." He said that the word has come to pass and fulfilled in our day that there would in the last days be a famine for hearing of the word of God.

Amos 8: 11

"Behold the days shall come, saith the Lord God, that I will send a famine in the Land, not a famine for bread, nor a thirst for water, but of hearing of the words of the lord"

People today would try and buy God or his favor as though God acted on a merit system and some preachers today are preying on this weakness in order to make fat their own pig. People will give to these ministers because they feel that they have done something to earn God's blessings when the word says we received his favor when we accepted his son into our lives and we became heirs of God.

God will not swat a fly off of our face when he gave us a hand to do it with ourselves. I said yes Paul, we cannot promise people that God will pay their bills and keep them from poverty when they got the health and the means to work and make the right decisions on how they spend their money. What we can promise them is that with Christ in their life, they do not have to go through the trials and experiences of life alone. He will go through it with them and bring them out and they can experience his love and peace even in the midst of adversity. The Preacher related to me of numerous stories of people in need writing to these ministries asking for help and being turned down when in fact they had been supporting these same ministers for years. If they were to receive a reply from one of the well known preachers to come and pray for them or a loved one, they would always demand a large sum of money to make the trip. I related to the Preacher that for the last few years, God has been dealing with my heart about compiling a book about the tithe and the right of the common people to eat the tithe in the church. The Preacher replied that he would have nothing to do with it stating that it was against church doctrine.

I have noticed though that the Lord has been softening his heart and dealing with my friend on this subject but that will be in another book. Paul stated that he is being directed by the lord to do a research on the right of the widows and the poor which is being ignored by the prosperity doctrine which is making the preachers rich while the culture around them is going to hell. He is already upset that some of these well known ministries have armed guards in their worship services. My friend is pretty upset with organized religion and so am I especially with preachers on TV stating that one needs to sow a seed into the Kingdom of God as a seed offering for God to do something needful in someone's life. They ask the people to send them their debts and they are going to have a special event where they will burn these bills as if they are burning the devils of poverty which caused the debts. What about the poor?

The Withered Hand

Paul believes he was the first recipient of the Withered Hand Ministry. Paul's hand was deformed at birth but the Spirit of the LORD moved upon his cradle and it became reformed to be normal. His grandmother often testified to this wondrous miracle gift of God.

Matthew 12:10-13

"And, behold, there was a man which had his hand withered. And they asked him, saying, Is it lawful to heal on the Sabbath days? That they might accuse him. Then saith he to the man, Stretch forth thine hand. And he stretched it forth; and it was restored whole, like as the other"

God was able to use Paul, even before he made a full comeback into ministry. He remembers compassionately praying for healing for someone he worked with who had poor circulation and lack of warmth in his feet and legs. God performed the healing.

Romans 11:29

"For the gifts and calling of God are without repentance."

Paul had a call with destiny if he would surrender his free will and come under submission to God. {Are you hiding from your calling in fear or unbelief? Are you losing countless sheep to Satan unnecessarily?}

God started turning up the ministry fires within him. Satan attacked Paul through church members. A group met with his pastor announcing that they would leave the church unless Paul was forbidden to preach.

He informed Paul of the rift in the church but told him he knew God was with him and he would not ask him to stop or to leave. His pastor's spirit was saddened by the controversy but did not ask him to preach from that day on.

Paul's preaching partner, The Intimidator, entered his life around this point. The Intimidator came from a Baptist background and their doctrine did not acknowledge spiritual gifts. The Intimidator had received the baptism with fire and hungered to learn more about the gift of speaking in tongues. He discussed his need to learn with a local Pentecostal pastor named Help. He inquired of the pastor how the evidence of the Holy Spirit took place. He told The Intimidator to go home and ask God. The Intimidator followed his advice, and began praying for the evidence and God blessed him with this wonderful gift as the beautiful language began flowing from his mouth. The Intimidator discussed this with his Baptist pastor and was not asked to perform any type of ministry for over a year. He realized that he would not be allowed to hold any position in this church and decided to resign his position and move on.

While searching for a different church to learn from, he attended the one Paul was attending. The Intimidator approached Paul after the service and they discussed the trucker-evangelist side of ministry. The Intimidator had met Mays Jackson, another trucker-evangelist and showed Paul brother Mays' signature in his Bible. Paul informed The Intimidator that brother Mays' was a well known radio personality with the truckers but probably had never driven one of the big rigs. Under the inspiration of the Holy Spirit, Paul snatched his bible and signed it too! The intimidator was astonished at Paul's boldness and was unsure how to deal with him.

He thought The Preacher was one of the most unusual people he had ever met. The Intimidator asked a pastor friend about Paul. He was told to stay away and that Paul had strange ways. Paul still had long hair and dressed in the western attire he prefers and was definitely different from most pastors at the time.

The burden of The Intimidator's own rejection was wearing on him and he came back to Paul's church despite the warning. The second night he visited, The Intimidator noticed Paul weeping and praising the LORD while enjoying the gospel singing and worship service. The Intimidator began to question why God no prayed and asked God to show him what was wrong. Later, He attended one of the miracle meetings Paul preached in Somewhere, VA. He later testified that it was like fresh oil being poured into his body, soul, and spirit. The feeling of refreshment helped him remember some of the spiritual heights he had experienced in the past. He felt healing in the spiritual void brought on by the hurts others had inflicted in his ministry. He felt it was a threefold message being preached in him at the same time but remaining distinct, easily understood. The Intimidator recognized a connection with Paul and left the church soon after Paul decided to. The LORD blessed Paul by increasing his radio ministry almost immediately. His broadcast was named "Standing for Jesus" because Paul wanted others to see God as he saw Him. He made a covenant with God to continue to minister in this venue if God would reveal Himself to others through it. Paul is convinced that we are living in the days of the rapture of the church. He believes that God is going to move on the church as a body, not just individuals, performing many mighty miracles. He believes that God will astonish the world at large: a last push for the "precious fruits" sake. We are all part of a great generation in the time when Israel has returned to their homeland and the Word of God has been published in almost every known language of the world.

Luke 1:17

"And He shall go before Him in the spirit and power of Elias, to turn the hearts of the fathers to the children, and the disobedient to the wisdom of the just; to make ready a people prepared for the Lord."

"...to make ready a people..." is the call of the body of Christ even now as this is being written for it is "...Maranatha." which means like it or not. The LORD comes.

Malachi 4:5-6

"Behold, I will send you Elijah the prophet before the coming of the great and dreadful day of the LORD: And he shall turn the heart of the fathers to the children, and the heart of the children to their fathers, lest I come and smite the earth with a curse."

"...The heart of the children to their fathers..." is the ministry laid to the body of Christ before the "dreadful day of the LORD." Under the direction of the Holy Spirit, Paul began broadcasting from a small station in Somewhere, TN. God used this broadcast to reconcile five churches in the area that had been quarreling among each other for some time. When God closes one door of opportunity, He always has another door for us to go through in His season of time. If your heart is with Him and is right with Him, you will not have to go through the door to the proverbial "woodshed." for chastisement, only doors of opportunity to serve Him.

Driving big rigs can bring you into contact with some wonderful people of God. Chaplain Mercy teaches drivers a simple, yet tremendously effective prayer she received from the Holy Spirit. She instructs them to begin with praise and worship of the LORD.

Then they ask the Heavenly Father to give them the load (shipment) that He had ordained for them to have so they may take the Holy Ghost where He is needed the most, and that in the end we would hear "Well done thou good and faithful servant." Another meeting with a man of God came when Paul was driving on interstate seventy-seven in one of the worst of snowstorms he had ever personally experienced.

There were wrecks everywhere! He had talked earlier with north bound drivers and was told the southbound lanes was closed ahead and he needed to reroute from US 460 to US 19 to reach interstate 81. This was a regular trucker's route so Paul felt confident in rerouting. The radio scratched with a man's shaken voice. He said, "Big truck, can I make it down seventy-seven to Wytheville (VA)?" Paul replied, "No you can't. The road is closed. There has been an accident. You'll have to follow me and cut back north on 81." The man's name was Temperance the Musician. Temperance and his wife Gentleness and their son Meekness were driving in the storm. During their conversation down US 460, Paul's gearshift broke off near the floorboard with only a nub left to shift with. He believes Satan meeting. Temperance owned a radio station in Somewhere, VA. The state police had called to tell Temperance that the roof of the station had caved in due to the weight of ice on it. They all made it through the storm to the radio station and temperance invited Paul to preach on his station after discussing the way God was using Paul in that type of ministry.

The LORD blessed Paul with a large radio audience. One day the Holy Spirit told Paul that there was going to be a great move of God, and to get ready for a revival that would be a miracle meeting to remember. Paul was super charged by the Holy Spirit as he prepared for this miracle meeting. Gentleness had been diagnosed with hardening of the arteries in her neck.

Plaque was destroying her brain. She was told that several surgeries would be needed to remove the blockages. The LORD gave Paul liberty to pray for her and her surgical prescreen testing showed no blockage! The surgeons were so baffled they made it a case study for the medical journals. Their typed report was nearly three pages full. Temperance testified of this event on a local television broadcast. As a gesture of their gratitude, Temperance and Gentleness gave Paul lifelong free broadcasts on their radio station. Paul still remembers the first time he preached on this station.

He called the station several weeks after their initial meeting and Temperance put him on the air while they were talking. He asked Paul to pray, so he did. People started calling in wwas. A few weeks later Paul was given a load to deliver near the area and called the station to let them know he would be available. Temperance was enthusiastic and picked him up at the exit. Paul was unsure of his sermon topic and the LORD gave him a message from the Song of Solomon, "He Still Loves Me!" Temperance recorded the sermon, without Paul's knowledge, and later used excerpts of it as an advertisement for his future broadcasts. The response to these excerpts was also very good and people responded over the phone and mailed several letters of encouragement and gratitude to Paul. One letter from a local pastor said that she had to pull their car over to weep sweet tears of joy along with her mother after hearing Paul's sermon. This same pastor was in television as well as radio and her contact led to Paul's television evangelism program. God had blessed him with three radio shows and one television program, all broadcasting during the same time period.

One overcast day, Paul was leaving a T.V. broadcast he had been visiting and was asked to give this pastor, Forgiveness, a ride home.

Paul was driving his pickup truck and it started raining before they left the building. He began placing his electric guitar and amp in the truck bed. Forgiveness told him to front but he knew there wouldn't be enough room for her and the equipment. He told her the equipment was God's to use for His Glory and if the rain ruined it, God would replace it with something better. He prayed for the equipment to remain safe and the rain stopped the moment he said A-men. Paul exclaimed, "God must not have wanted His equipment hurt" and smiled at forgiveness. He later met another friend of Temperance, a brother in Christ named Help and his wife Charity.

Help later met Paul at a local truck stop and brought him to meet his wife Charity at their home. She was in poor condition with heart disease and was not expected to survive long. Paul prayed for her and she was miraculously healed. Help and Charity still testify that they would drive a hundred miles to hear Paul preach. They were very moved by the "He Still Loves Me" broadcast as well. Help and Charity invited Paul to stay at their home while the Virginia miracle meetings were in progress. The LORD led Paul to pray for each of these dear people sometime before the miracle meetings were held and Help was healed of cancer, Charity was healed of heart disease and their granddaughter was healed of diabetes. Charity's daughter, Courage, came to Paul with a prayer request for healing of her ankles and knees so she could attend church. Paul felt the jolt of Spiritual virtue running down his arm into her ankles as he laid hands on them and prayed. Paul was showering around an hour later and heard excited shouts downstairs. His curiosity aroused, Paul dressed quickly and descended the stairs. When Courage spotted him, she asked him to stick his finger up and move it from side to side. He played along and she let out a shrill of praise and ran through the house on her newly healed ankles.

Help and Charity explained that she had been in an auto accident. She was an EMT (Emergency Medical Technician) riding in the rear of an ambulance when the driver fell asleep at the wheel and hit two parked cars. Courage ran back through the house shouting that her eyes were free! The accident had broken nearly every bone in her body and her eyes had been left paralyzed from the ordeal. Her recovery took many months and her knees, ankles and eyes had remained damaged. Her fixed eyes had kept her from getting a driver's license and from any gainful employment. She fully recovered after Paul's prayer and was happily married.

Courage's daughter, Promise had terrible grades and hated school. She had problems concentrating and was failing her classes. Her mother's near fatal accident had traumatized her and Paul felt this was part of her problem. The Holy Spirit told Paul to pray for her and tell her she was going to college with the continued direction of the Spirit. She graduated among the top of her class and is now enrolled in college with a major in psychiatry. During a revival Paul preached in Virginia, a man came through the door limping because he had a nail puncture wound in his foot.

After a few steps in the door, he testified that he was completely healed without a trace of the wound left behind. Another highlight, at the same revival, was the night the local fire department showed up. They didn't come to worship but in response to a report from neighbors that the church was on fire. The firemen testified that they could see flames surrounding the church from the roadside below. The only flame there, however, was that of the Holy Spirit's precious engulfing presence. Their testimony spread throughout the community and surrounding churches.

THE DEVIL'S NIGHT OUT
(Several instances of the "casting out" of demons)

On the third night of a revival in Somewhere, Virginia later referred to as the miracle meetings, a woman at the pulpit began speaking in tongues but it sounded more like a tormented chant. The previous night, the same lady sat behind Paul and he heard terrible slurs of cursing, in a male voice, spewing from her. The Holy Spirit informed Paul it was the same woman who had called his radio show, a couple of months prior to this revival, asking for deliverance from a problem. Paul instructed her on the air not to tell him her problem for the LORD had already revealed it and he would be praying for her. As she stood at the altar of the church, Paul asked her plainly, "Are you ready to be free of them devils?" She said, "I thought God was never going to show you. YES!" Paul slung his guitar behind him and grabbed her by the head as God instructed him in an open vision (instructing him as it happened) to do. He demanded that the demons come out of her. Brother Encouragement and the pastor joined in. The ensuing commotion, along with the wicked male voice speaking through her mouth, scared several members of the congregation into observing events from the outside. The demon-empowered woman was able to knock Paul up against the wall, but fell down screaming and convulsing as Paul commanded the entity to leave in the name of Jesus. The Elder Brother Encouragement finally was able to overcome it by the Holy Spirit within him and his ministerial experience in demonic areas. This was Paul's first encounter with demons and it scared him tremendously. Brother Encouragement took authority over this thing in the name of JESUS! It left the church and the congregation timidly filed back in to continue the service.

On the ride home with the Help family, they noticed a black raven flying along the same route they were traveling. When they arrived home, the raven flew directly to the upstairs window of Paul's room and began pecking sharply on the window. The LORD revealed to Paul that the demon had left the woman and went into the bird. God gave him a prophetic gesture in the form of burning the tape of the earlier meeting, once this was accomplished; the bird flew away and did not return.

Matthew 8:31-32

"So the devils besought Him, saying, If thou cast us out, suffer us to go away into the herd of swine... And He said unto them, Go."

On one trip with the Help family to Panther, WV, Paul was exhausted from driving a long run and was resting his eyes during the ride. The LORD gave him a vision of a woman standing outside the church door, wanting desperately to enter but unable to. Paul shared the vision with Help and Charity. As the church was filling up for the service, a woman peered inside but did not enter. Paul said, "Well, just let her stay out there. It'll be alright." Paul ministered to those wanting prayer after the message. One woman stood to give a message in tongues and the interpretation came through Paul; stating that a man in the church wanted to destroy it. The women of the church were given a prophetic gesture from the interim pastor to remove their shoes and gather into a circle to pray. Suddenly, it was as if someone had spit into Paul's hair, when he noticed that he was the only one at the altar left standing. A wind of God had blown through and most everyone else was lying on the floor, slain in the spirit. Paul noticed a couple of men approaching through the middle aisle. These men also became slain in the spirit as Paul stood in amazement at the altar. They fell to the floor with their legs and arms pointing straight up in the air!

Paul was told later that these men were planning to do him harm as well as burn the church to the ground. The leader of the group's wife was the one unable to enter the church. The group remained on the floor for the rest of the service. When it ended, the wife came in from the porch and the men repented and became Christians.

Another woman came from back of the church and walked directly towards Paul. She began to rock back and forth, praying aloud when God spoke through her in the voice of a man. She testified of Paul's prophetic call, his life and of his relationship with his wife. She reminded him of the anointing God had placed upon him and how Paul was holding Him back from using him. She told him to get busy in the work of the LORD and to stop entering in and going out. The Holy Spirit quickened Paul's understanding and he realized that she was referring to the gift of praying in tongues. He had been experimenting up to this time but needed to become serious in exercising this gift. God's Spirit was taking control of his actions and words in the ministry. No one at the church knew who the lady was and they were unsuccessful in locating her anywhere in or near the church. On another occasion, Paul was in Pennsylvania when Charity called to tell him that both she and Help were to be hospitalized. The Holy Spirit came upon Paul and he said, "No you're not, I'll be there in the morning. Come pick me up and we'll watch God move." Charity had seen so many miracles around Paul's prayers that she came in faith to pick him up the next morning. In their living room, he prayed for Help and Charity when their future daughter-in-law came in the room. God revealed to Paul that a demon was tormenting her. With more experience in this area of ministry, he was able to cast out the foul spirit and saw a shadow go into the laundry room adjacent to the living room.

The Word of the LORD spoke through Paul and told him that the demon had entered into their washer and dryer and they would never work again, and it never did.

On the way out of the house the word of the LORD came upon Paul and he told Charity the Lord was going to bless her house for opening up their home to him in order to do the Virginia revival. He revealed that there was a big package on the way and it would consist of everything she had needed for a while. Within a month, UPS delivered an enormous package to Charity's home. It was addressed to her and did not have a return address or an invoice inside. Her husband feared there would be a large bill to pay, and that it was a gimmick of some kind. Two months passed and Charity finally opened the box and it contained towels, dishes, pots and pans, cleaning supplies, and etc. "Everything she needed...she never received an invoice." The Intimidator, Paul's preaching partner, held a revival at Pastor Longing's church in Somewhere, TN. Paul was a chartered member of the church and was visiting on this occasion in support of his friend. A young man came forward for prayer to release him from demonic possession. Pastor Longing asked Paul to help because this was a new experience for him with demonic forces. It turned out that there was more than one demon in the man and they began to jerk his body around the church. They banged his head on the floor and Pastor Longing placed his hands underneath the man's head to avoid injury.

Pastor Longing was trying to talk to this young man, but he began to wail. Paul told Pastor Longing, "That isn't him talking; it's the demons in him." Sister Waiting, the pastor's wife, grabbed the anointing oil and poured it all over her hands. After laying hands on the young man, she began to pray for him. The other young men of the church tried to hold him down to no avail.

Paul told them to let him go! He spoke to the demons controlling the boy, "Devil's, you know who I am and whom I serve! And you will bow to the man of God." Paul then called on the Angels of God to come and smite these tormenting spirits with the full wrath of God.

To everyone's amazement, suddenly some unseen force literately picked the man up from the floor, turned him face down in mid-air and then slammed him to the floor in front of Paul The Preacher. , "Paul said, Devil, I am just about tired of dealing with you! Name yourselves in the name of JESUS I command you!" One by one they named themselves; murder, hate, lust, etc... Murder and hate were the only ones that put up a fight. Paul charged the warring angels of heaven to leave the throne room of God in the name of JESUS, to come and "cut" these stubborn demons from the boy, since the demons would not heed the man of God's commands.

The demons were forced from the young man. His face contorted in agony and he groaned and wailed as they left. (Sister Glowing of a well known tape ministry was also present at this bone chilling event.) She stated that she had never witnessed anything like this before!

Mark 9:25-29

"When Jesus saw that the people came running together, He rebuked the foul spirit, saying unto him, Thou dumb and deaf spirit, I charge thee, come out of him, and enter no More into him. and the spirit cried, and rent him sore, and came out of him: and he was as one dead; insomuch that many said, he is dead. But Jesus took him by the hand, and lifted him up; and he arose. And when He was come into the house, His disciples asked him privately, Why could not we cast him out? And He said unto them, This kind can come forth by nothing, but by prayer and fasting."

Paul visited the young man at his home and the Spirit told him that there had been a murder committed in the house. The young man replied that there had been three that he knew of. In the Spirit, Paul could see a figure of flesh and blood walking through the house with an upraised knife, as if ready to strike.

Pastor Longing later called Paul to come to his home and view a computer digital picture taken in the house where the young boy lived. The picture showed the demon following him from the bathroom with an upraised knife in its hand. This was the same entity the Holy Spirit had revealed to Paul. The three pastors prayed over the house and after the young man testified to others, the full scope of these combined events convicted the youth in the area to burn all the books and musical records they could find pertaining to witchcraft. Later several of the young teenagers announced their call to ministry.

Acts 19:19-20

"Many of them also which used curious arts brought their books together, and burned them before all men: So mightily grew the word of God and prevailed."

18 Wheels and Jesus

Brother Encouragement, Paul and members of several other churches held a tent revival in Somewhere, VA. To Paul's amazement, People came from every denomination conceivable, praying for God to move in their lives and at the meetings. A sudden windstorm began to stir and a large whirlwind came up under the tent directly in front of the pulpit where Paul was standing. The small twister gathered papers off the seats into its funnel. The fear of God fell in the place. A man named Destruction, who had previously threatened to do harm the home of Help and Charity, ran to them and started begging them for their forgiveness. The force of the wind was so strong; it drove all completely outside the tent. Everyone ran outside to help others up and the wind calmed down, nearly as suddenly as it began. Someone cried, "Hey Look up in the Sky!" There were three crosses shining through the stars, etched in the sky. God allowed them to outwardly see his blessings. The air was supercharged with the power of God as a truck driver and his wife came forward for prayer. The LORD filled Paul with His Holy Spirit and Power. When he began praying for the couple, the power of God entered and they fell motionless to the floor. The woman was around 8 months pregnant at the time. A person later made a comment to Paul, "Man, this has got to be real! There is no way that woman could have went down like that and been all right! And you didn't even touch them!" The Preacher said, "Oh Yes, It's as real as it gets!" During that same meeting, one of the visiting Baptist preachers prayed for relief from his battle with his addiction to cigarettes. His church was planning a revival for the next week and he did not want the burden of his conscience to interfere with the meetings. He was slain in the spirit as soon as Paul began praying for him and he began speaking in tongues while lying in the grass. He preached an awesome sermon when he was able to get up!

The next day, a pastor of another area church named Hunger asked Paul to meet him before the evening service. He wanted Paul to help him pray for the sick. Paul eagerly agreed and they drove to the local hospital. A young lady in this Pastor's congregation had taken an overdose of pills. She was brain dead and the hospital was waiting for the family to sign the release papers to unplug her life support. Paul said, "Pastor Hunger, what in the world do you want me to do? She's dead!" He replied, "PRAY! She died in a bad way. Who can tell where she will end up! Just pray for her, Preacher!" Paul asked God to restore her sanity and to send her spirit back into her body from wherever it had gone to. The intensive care unit allows 4-minute visitations only. Pastor Hunger wanted to visit other church members in the hospital so Paul waited for him in the lounge. He stood near a small end table meditating on the LORD and began praying. The lighting in the room was subdued and he was trying to read a Gideon Bible opened on the table when a bright light beamed down on the Bible to highlight this verse: Isaiah 60:1

"Arise, shine; for thy light is come, and the glory of the LORD is risen upon thee."

Pastor Hunger walked in shortly afterwards to exclaim, "MY GOD! Preacher, God is in this place!" Paul said, "I know He just walked in a minute ago." They began to praise and worship God together. Pastor Hunger wanted to pray once more for a man in ICU before they left. On their way back to the room, Paul noticed a lot of activity around the curtain of the woman that they had just prayed for and wanted to ask a nurse what was all the activity. Pastor Hunger tried in vain to stop him stating that they had probably taken her off life support and that she was deceased. Paul asked a nurse what was going on and she replied, "She's alive! She regained consciousness pulling the tubes out not knowing where she was and she wants something to eat.

We don't understand. Emotions run high when God moves in a personal way. The medical personnel were unable to explain her recovery and were convinced she would have permanent brain damage and many physical problems from the overdose. Jesus had a different ending to the story and she was able to fully recover both physically and mentally. Paul had been in quiet prayer in the upstairs bedroom at brother Help's home before the next meeting. He learned that a sister in the LORD, hundreds of miles away, had been stricken with cancer. She was bedridden and near death. Paul attempted to call and pray for her but the line was cut off before the connection was made. This happened three times. The gift of discernment came alive in him and he realized that Satan, the enemy, was attacking the effort. Paul tried in vain to call the radio station in order to get some help praying for her. The connection was severed three times before he was able to get through. Paul fell to his knees in the corner of the room to pray and do spiritual battle. He was finally able to get through, both in the natural and supernatural. Sometime later, the woman and her family later attended a concert in Somewhere, VA to see Paul. She testified that she immediately received back her strength while talking with Paul on the phone. The oncologist ran tests and reported that there was no cancer left in her body! Her husband and a friend had traveled with her to the concert. The friend asked Paul to pray for healing of her cleft lip that disfigured her face. In the boldness of the anointing upon Paul's life, he covered her mouth with his hand and prayed. When he removed his hand, God had healed her instantly! What a God of love! All things are possible to them that believe. Another incident that occurred in an ICU setting involved a friend of Paul's. He was near death but had lived a long life and knew the Lord. Paul knew he would miss him but felt the nearness of God's presence in the room and it brought comfort to him. Another occupant of the ICU was a dying mother.

In the waiting room Paul overheard the young man whimpering over his mother. She was in a coma and was unresponsive at the time. The Spirit of the LORD came upon Paul and he felt engulfed with compassion for them both. Moved by this tremendous power of pure love, Paul walked over and tapped the young man on the shoulder. When he looked up, Paul asked him softly if he could sit with him.

He received a muffled reply and sat down. Paul began letting the Lord use him to help build up this young man's faith by sharing some of the ways that the Living God had used him to touch others. He asked the Holy Spirit for guidance and asked the young man to pray with him. He agreed distractedly and Paul began, "God, I ask you please to manifest yourself in me and in this prayer. God I can feel the compassion this young man has for his momma, and God, I can feel your compassion for him. So Father, I just ask you, to reach wherever this woman's spirit is and to restore it back to her body and with this LORD I also ask you to restore her body and heal whatever has been damaged so that she can be in her right mind and right bodily functions for food, drink and more. Let this boy and his mother have a few more years' together, because you know God, this boy's not ready yet for her to go. Paul closed his prayer with "Thank-you God for hearing me, Amen.

Paul then walked out. The next day as Paul walked into the ICU department, the young man, his pastor and a few other people jumped to their feet when they saw him. The young man was smiling broadly and said, "Mister, I don't know who you are, but your feet had not even hit the pavement, as to what my mother came to herself, in her right mind, and wanting something to drink, and she has asked to meet you but before you meet her I feel led to tell you the whole story!

Several months ago, momma had been in an awful accident several states over that left her in a coma.

They transported her back here just a few weeks ago, and today the doctors were going to unplug her life support because they felt that there was no hope and that all the tests indicated if she ever did recover she would have been a paraplegic with severe brain damage. And now, none of that's true. She's sitting up in bed and is just like she used to be! Our whole family want to Thank you mister, thank-you..." embracing Paul. The Preacher assured him that he only prayed and Jesus did all the healing. Paul and I hope through the work and prayer that has gone into this novel that you will open your mind to the possibility that there is an Almighty God who loves each and every one of us and is not willing for any to perish? God is special! He deserves special treatment! He wants to fulfill His word and promises through and in everyone who will give all of themselves totally over to Him!

Romans 2:11

"For there is no respect of persons with God"

WE learn in this novel that God is the special one, not Paul The Preacher. We humans are but vessels to be used. We can either be filled to pour out the things of God and His kingdom, or the things of Satan and his quickly failing existence. May the LORD grant us the wisdom to know what it is that is being poured into our spirit and out of our life! We need to pray for others to receive the Holy drink of His Spirit of Love and Joy in the Holy Ghost!

Mouse Under The Chair
(Where The Nightmare Began)

The Preacher was en-route with a load to Georgia and it was well after midnight. Paul had been praying for several hours concerning financial matters that His radio and television ministries were having. He had been praying earnestly over this and his ministry partners when The Lord gave him a word. The Lord spoke to him telling how that some of the preachers on this particular radio station were no longer preaching judgmentally with an iron fist, but rather was now preaching in the love of Christ.

The Lord had touched them through Paul's ministry and caused them to change their preaching style. Paul replied, "Lord I will stay on the air even if I have to pay for it out of my\own pocket." That same day around lunch Paul's satellite communications beeped in his truck. The very owner of the company had written Paul informing him that he was to come see him when he arrived at the terminal. Paul was thinking his boss was going to force him to remove the crosses from his truck and his ministry tapes from the driver's lounge. He decided to resign if this was the case. His boss shocked him when he asked about his television and radio programs. Stunned Paul replied, "Well you see it's like this- I once was blind but now I see! I was lost but now I'm saved!" He said, "No Paul, what I want to know is how much is it costing for you to have them. You see, I've been watching you over the years and I believe in you. I just don't have any confidence in any of the others. All they seem to ever want is money, and I have never once heard you ask for a dime! Just the other day, I saw you on T.V. and liked what I saw. I want to pay for one of your broadcasts that I might be apart of what you are doing.

Later, Paul found out that his boss had CEO's of large corporations listen to his chaplain driver minister on one of the local radio stations. The Preacher soon met a pastor who seemed to be a Godsend. Their personalities meshed right away and he asked for Paul's help in the leadership of his church. Paul's heart belonged to his home church. He discussed the situation with them and received their blessing before he agreed to help the other church. Paul had served in a helping role for a little while when the pastor's wife became ill and was near death in the hospital. Paul visited her and was given a vision of a baby, wearing blue, reaching down for her. He didn't have the interpretation from God, only the vision, so he described it to her. Some months after her death, his pastor associate told him she had miscarried a boy years before and had never stopped grieving for him. The vision God gave Paul had brought peace to her soul before she died. Trouble began when Paul included this pastor in his current ministries on the air. Over time, this pastor began belittling others in the ministry and tried to usurp Paul's position as leader.

Eventually, his condescending attitude and actions toward others interested in the radio and television programs became such an issue that Paul decided to cancel them all. Paul learned a hard lesson on following his heart and the peace that comes with God's blessings!

Note:
Our character, Paul The Preacher is sometimes given instruction from God to ask for healing or for comfort or to warn others of the toll sin will take in their lives. He can't heal anyone; he can only follow what God tells him to do. Healing is like a radio transmission. There is the transmitter, an antenna or coax, and a receiver.

The transmitter is God, the antenna or coax is the minister who acquires the signal and becomes a conduit for the receiver, and the receiver is the person with the need who tunes in the signal by their faith to manifest what the transmitter has sent.

This, however, was certainly not the end of The Preacher's ministry. It continues on from truck stop to truck stop, dock-to-dock, small chapels and many churches. Everlasting was one of Paul's mentors in the ministry, and a good friend as well. Everlasting was a very successful businessman who was saved in his later years. He left his thriving career to enter into ministry. A sermon of his titled *"Mouse Under the Chair"* is one of Paul's favorites. Everlasting began the sermon by describing a couple that was fortunate enough to be invited to the inauguration of the Queen of England. They were in the middle of the entire splendor surrounding the event: flags, polished uniforms, shiny trumpets, gold, glitter, and etc. When they returned from their excursion someone asked, "How was it? What did you see?" They snapped back with, "We saw a mouse under the chair of the Queen!" Can you imagine traveling that far, scheduling connections, travel arrangements and being blessed to see the royal ceremonies and the only thing they remembered was a mouse under the chair? It's like some of the people attending church now; they can only find fault in the most ridiculous things and not be blessed to be in the center of the splendor of worshipping God. Satan will do anything to distract your mind, emotions and your heart from seeking the living God. We enter a congregation of the saints, where the Spirit of God is moving mightily in His Splendor and all we see is the mouse under the chair. Whatever it may be that distracts you from the movement of God falls into Satan's agenda to steal, kill and destroy you by his deception and distractions. Everlasting had given Paul a song idea to be titled "It Won't Always Be This Way."

Paul recently asked a friend, Enduring, to rewrite and record the song. Enduring is the Pastor of Music with a large Trucking Ministry. He had written a ballad about The Preacher's ministry titled "18 Wheels and Jesus" before they met. Enduring is also friends with Temperance and had heard of the miracle for Gentleness that God had used Paul to intercede in.

Enduring traveled to Brownstown, IL to sing at a jamboree at the Road Angel Trucker Center.

Another friend of Paul's, named Awakened, was in Illinois at this gathering and heard Enduring sing "18 Wheels and Jesus." Awakened called Paul to tell him someone had written a song about his life and ministry. Awakened gave Enduring the phone number to reach Paul and they found out that they lived three miles apart in the same town. God sent Enduring to Illinois to meet Paul, who lived across the hill! Paul was blessed to witness more awesome miracles of God at a little Baptist church in Kentucky. Pastor Steadfast had seen God's almighty hand upon Paul's life at the Christian Retreat. He asked Paul to preach a service for him. He arrived while the others were in Sunday school and proceeded to anoint the sanctuary with oil, continuously saying "The Blood of Jesus" as he walked around the room. He preached a sermon titled "What good's the wedding without the wine." He preached, "A lot of churches don't want the God of the Bible in their services, but would rather have God left back in the Sunday school room." He reminded them that Jesus turned the water into wine and borrowing part of a sermon preached by his friend Everlasting, told them that when the Lord of the Universe told the servants to bring water and put it into the vessels, the water "blushed" before its Creator and became wine. Continuing on, Paul stated that humans don't have enough reverence to bow and blush before Christ and wonder why they don't have the "wine" of the Holy Spirit in their life or in their church.

It appears that the wedding would have been an embarrassment for the groom and his family if Jesus had not provided the wine when they ran out. How much will we, as individuals be embarrassed before God if we have not submitted our life to God beginning with the supernatural change of being "born again"? He can turn our vessels of plain water into heavenly wine that will last throughout eternity for the wedding of the church and the bridegroom, Jesus Christ.

God blessed The Preacher with the gift to read the hearts of two ladies that morning. Pastor Steadfast knew the information had to be sent by God because Paul had not met either woman. After church, inspired by this demonstration of God's power and knowledge, Steadfast took Paul throughout the community to visit former members of the church who no longer attended. Paul did not want to be aware of the problems in these people's lives. God would show him and he would tell them what God had revealed to him. When they finally returned to the church, there were several people waiting for them. There were two preachers who begged to be let in. They had backslid in their walk with God and knew that the end would come and they would not be ready to go. One of them came forward during the closing invitation to be anointed with oil and prayed for. Paul asked how much oil he wanted to be used. He responded, "However the Lord leads you." The Lord led Paul to anoint him with almost half the bottle of oil and he willingly received it all. Why was this backsliding preacher so willing? God had manifested Himself through The Preacher in his sermon on Heaven, "... Picture with me, at this wedding supper of Christ and His bride, we are all going to be seated and Jesus will personally serve us each individually the wine and the manna. With joyful anticipation, we watch as He serves each one at the table. When it is our turn, we ask to serve Him instead and He replies, "No! I've been waiting a long time for this.

I saw you when you were doing without. I saw when you lived by faith when you did not have the means to go. When it was cold, you drove by homes glowing with warmth and you felt that no one cared. You went to visit the sick "sheep" for me. I wanted to leave heaven then and wrap you in my arms, but I was constrained by the Father's will. I brought your name up before our Father that moment and we went over the plan for your life again.

As we discussed your end and the glory you would bring His Kingdom; I envisioned myself serving you this day, "This is my honor and time to serve you." Paul continued, "Dear friend, if you look close I believe you will see a tear in Jesus eyes." Members of the congregation were standing in the pews at this point, trying to see Jesus. When the altar call was given, many souls made their way to the front to get their life in order with His will.

Then the Lord spoke to Paul and said He wanted to fill some vessels. (Which means that He was going to baptize some with the power and boldness of God's Spirit?) Paul said, "God, not in here, this is a Baptist church. They don't believe in this." (Paul did not know that the founding Pastor of this church had received this wondrous gift of God, and their current Pastor, Steadfast, had also received this gift at the Christian Retreat some months before}. Paul told the congregation what God had told him and invited those whom God was leading to come forward. A man came to the front and stood before Paul. The Lord flashed a vision to him of the man's left ear, his right hand, right foot, right knee and stomach area also. Paul said, "Brother, I don't understand why God is showing me what He is, but I believe I'll just obey God." He began anointing each place God had shown him in the vision. Paul had barely touched his ear when the man suddenly started talking in a beautiful language. Immediately, Pastor Steadfast was slain in the Spirit and was also speaking in tongues.

(Being slain in the spirit, lying on the floor, was very much out of character for Steadfast). Many others came forward and Jesus would spiritually baptize them and they all were blessed with the gift of stammering lips. Then the man whose ear Paul had touched began to shout and to cry at the same time. He kept opening and closing his fist and hopping up and down. He was able to compose himself after a period of time and said, "You don't know it, but everyone here in this room does.

I was born without eardrums but I can hear you now! I read your lips before, but now I hear you! I was injured every place you touched me in a car accident and God has made me whole. I couldn't even make a fist before, for a long time, but now look!" He opened and squeezed his hand with a smile of relief and great joy. Eleven souls received the baptism of the Holy Ghost that night and Steadfast asked Paul to preach in an upcoming revival.

Isaiah 61:1

"The Spirit of the Lord GOD is upon me; because the LORD hath anointed me to preach good tidings unto the meek; He hath sent me to bind up the brokenhearted, to proclaim liberty to the captives, and the opening of the prison to them that are bound"

God moved greatly during these revivals. Paul's revival was called a "Spiritual Awakening." One of the messages that touched many women across the nation was titled "Leave The Light On In The Basement." Paul described a large chandelier in an entrance hall of a big house that was beautiful and bright. It was the little light in the basement, however, that kept you from falling and being injured when you had to get into the cellars of life and its light was important too. Paul asked them which of those lights did they want to be which caused several people to rethink their position in ministry.

The last night of the revival, Paul described a previous vision he had received of a Big Ben alarm clock with big bells on top of a round face. He found a similar one at Wal-Mart and was giving the altar call, waving that clock around, telling everyone that his or her time was just about to run out. He stressed their need to come to the altar and get their lives right with God. During the altar call, a white mouse ran between Paul's legs, under the pews and back and then disappeared.

This infuriated the man of God and he cursed the mouse and Satan for trying to distract God's children who were willing to lay their lives upon the altar of God's grace and mercy. The next day, a member causing trouble for Pastor Steadfast was the one God allowed to find the dead mouse on the altar. Paul believes it was symbolic of the fact that others in the church needed to get to Jesus and die to their self will. Paul had told Pastor Steadfast before the service began that a woman would be sitting in a certain section of the church and that she would have a controlling spirit. Paul felt her cast a spell against his life to bring him into a nightmare existence. He asked God to send the evil curse back to the source and to have His vengeance on the one who spoke it against him. Paul kept fighting this spirit and claiming the atonement and finished work of Christ.

Paul informed the spirit that the precious bloodshed by the Lord Jesus was a separator and protector from the enemy and that Satan had no grounds to be there with his continuous attacks against him. It was not long that Paul received word that the same lady that God had warned him about before church that night had died confirming Paul's suspicions that she was the spell caster.

Where Eagles Fly

God showered tremendous blessings at truck stop revivals that Paul will never forget. One example occurred at a Jesus Jamboree held by Chaplain Mercy. She had asked Paul to preach for her and the Holy Spirit confirmed his need to go. Paul's dispatcher scheduled a run shipping "just-in-time" automotive freight from Michigan to New Jersey and back again. This would normally be a grueling run, driving close to seven hundred miles a day. Paul was blessed with amazing stamina throughout the entire three week period. He would arrive every night at the truck stop and preach under the tent, this included all day Saturday and Sunday. One Saturday Paul preached on Eagles. Paul was unaware at the time, but a pair of Eagles had flown down from the mountain and circled the area behind him while he was preaching. The drivers testified that they circled during the entire sermon. When the sermon ended, the eagles drifted off and a tractor-trailer came in behind Paul. The loud noise of his air breaks attracted some attention. Paul glanced up to see one of the largest murals of an eagle that he had ever seen painted on the side of the truck. He pointed to a driver and said, "I can't keep preaching until I deliver this message from the Holy Ghost to you sir, God says He sees your broken heart and feels your pain. If you will put Him first you can have your home back." Paul had never met this man and he knew nothing about him. He talked with the man after the sermon and found out that he had left his truck with thoughts of suicide because his wife had filed for a divorce and his home was in foreclosure. Months later, the driver called Paul at home to tell him that he had held on to the "word" that God gave him to deliver and he had become a preacher after his home had been restored. To God be the Glory! This is a prime example of evangelism stretching forth through the power of Christ.

He said, "Preacher, now I'm one of those eagles dropping pieces of fresh meat to other eagles on the ground who are going through their times of molting, bringing encouragements so they too can be renewed.

Psalms 103:1-5

"Bless the LORD, O my soul: and all that is within me, bless his holy name. Bless the LORD, O my soul, and forget not all his benefits: Who forgiveth all thine iniquities; who healeth all thy diseases; Who redeemeth thy life from destruction; who crowneth thee with loving kindness and tender mercies; Who satisfieth thy mouth with good things; so that thy youth is renewed like the eagles".

Another example of God's blessings flowing during a truck stop revival is a driver who had lost his family. His wife was filing for a divorce and his in-laws had him arrested for molesting his children (a false accusation). He also had left his truck planning to kill himself. God gave Paul a similar verse for him. Paul met him later and was told that he too had held onto the word from God delivered by The Preacher. The false charges against him for molesting his children were dropped. While in the Judge's chambers, discussing the level of child support he needed to give, his wife fell back in love with him and the divorce was canceled.

The Love of God

The Preacher and I share Our inner thoughts... "How God knows me. How He knew me. How He has already seen my near and distant future. He has already seen me in heaven! I do not know how He is going to accomplish this. It is beyond my imagination. Beyond the expansion of my finite mind to know and to understand how He is going to bring me out of this fiery trial that I have been going through. But I know that He will."

1 Peter 4:12-13

"Beloved, think it not strange concerning the fiery trial which is to try you, as though some strange thing happened unto you".

The Preacher Continues... "God has not anointed me so highly (to His glory) for Him to leave me in such a state that is not of my own doing. The proceeding pages have testified to the blessed hope which I have and the zealousness of my confidence in His sure timing. He will not leave you nor forsake you. He has already seen you make it too. What would the people of the world give for such hope and assurance that comes freely with a personal relationship with Christ Jesus by faith realized?"

Hebrews 11:1

"Now faith is the substance of things hoped for, the evidence of things not seen."

Hebrews 10:22

"Let us draw near with a true heart in full assurance of faith, having our hearts sprinkled from an evil conscience, and our bodies washed with pure water."

I got happy and made mention to The Preacher that the people of the world look everywhere for this...everywhere...but only a few find it. They find it only in the person of Jesus the Christ. They find it on a path that is sound and narrow, leading to the only door of complete spiritual satisfaction. They find it only at the foot of the cross on Calvary's hill.

Matthew 7:13-14

"Enter ye in at the strait gate: for wide is the gate, and broad is the way, that leadeth to destruction, and many there be which go in thereat: Because strait is the gate, and narrow is the way, which leadeth unto life, and few there be that find it."

Instead of looking to the great bloody sacrifice of Christ's substitution payment for our individual personal sin, people will look to every other hilltop that does not reveal but rather tries to conceal their life, to no avail. It may seem an easier path for the moment; ever seeking, but never finding the "joy unspeakable and full of glory" that comes with that dreadful climb and awful beholding of the price that Jesus paid for them individually. Instead, some temporary pleasures of the sensual mind and flesh that flies away as quickly as a blast of wind, or may even last a long season, will hold their souls. They will not take heed to the fact that the end without Jesus is eternal death with agony beyond comprehension. One day, we will wake up to "...sleep no more." Our eternal existence will be judged. We all have the choice for either eternal life with the LORD Jesus Christ, with all the good things that matter, or eternal death where there is wailing and gnashing of teeth. Worse yet is the eternal separation from a God of mercy and peace and love that did not want you to go to such an awful place, but you failed to heed warning, after warning, after warning to escape. The Preacher Replied by quoting scripture!

Matthew 18:1-9

"At the same time came the disciples unto Jesus, saying, Who is the greatest in the kingdom of heaven? And Jesus called a little child unto Him, and set him in the midst of them, and said, Verily I say unto you, Except ye be converted, and become as little children, ye shall not enter into the kingdom of heaven. Whosoever therefore shall humble himself as this little child, the same is greatest in the kingdom of heaven. and whosoever shall receive one such little child in my name receiveth me. But whosoever shall offend one of these little ones which believe in me, it were better for him that a millstone were hanged about his neck, and that he were drowned in the depth of the sea".

I replied to The Preacher that rather intense are the forebodings of Christ's words as He teaches on the seriousness of avoiding hell's price. As this teaching continues, look at the love that comes forth...

Matthew 18:10-14

"Take heed that ye despise not one of these little ones; for I say unto you, That in heaven their angels do always behold the face of my Father which is in heaven. For the Son of man is come to save that which was lost. How think ye? if a man have an hundred sheep, and one of them be gone astray, doth he not leave the ninety and nine, and goeth into the mountains, and seeketh that which is gone astray? And if so be that he find it, verily I say unto you, he rejoiceth more of that sheep, than of the ninety and nine, which went not astray. Even so it is not the will of your Father which is in heaven, that one of these little ones should perish."

The Preacher Replied, Little Silas, how True are the next words of Jesus brought to full luminous view from all that has been revealed in this book?

John 3:16

"For God so loved the world, that He gave His only begotten Son, that whosoever believeth in Him should not perish, but have everlasting life."

Air Conditioned Salvation

Paul has experienced many manifestations of the Holy Spirit while driving. His truck had broken down in Rochester, NY and he was scheduled to run with two different drivers in their trucks. One driver did not know Jesus' name except to use as a curse word. The other driver was a Christian who had turned his back on Jesus. Paul remembers saying to the wayward Christian, "What's God going to have to do? Have a big truck pull up with a sign on it telling you Jesus loves you?" The driver tapped him on the shoulder and pointed to a tractor-trailer passing behind

Paul with those very words painted on the side. The other driver was not interested in anything Paul had to say about God. Paul continued to witness to him during the trip and the next summer their paths crossed again in Mobil, AL. He said, "Preacher, you may not have thought I wasn't listening coming down from Rochester, but it's like those words you spoke to me are haunting me. I can't get them out of my head. All the time I hear them, about being born again. I tell you what; my air conditioner has quit. (The temperature was over 100 degrees at the time.) If your God can fix my air conditioner, then I'll get saved." Paul had not faced such a direct challenge before and he said, "I don't know that He will, but I know that He can! Let's see!" The Preacher prayed, "You heard him LORD. Almighty God, there's a soul in the balance here. I know some preachers say that you can't enter into mechanical operations. But I believe you are all powerful and that you loved man so much that you let your own son suffer so we could be saved. I am asking you God, just let this air conditioner work 'till this poor lost soul gets to Tennessee, so he too will experience the God that I know and be saved." The A/C started to cool and continued to work the entire trip back to Tennessee.

The Shop foreman was unable to understand how it worked because the expansion valve was bad and leaking and there was not enough coolant left in the system to be operational. The driver was true to his word and received Jesus as his LORD and Savior! A lady in the safety department at work called Paul later to thank him for leading her future husband to the Lord. She had been attracted to him for a long time but would not pursue the relationship because he was not a Christian. A few months later, Paul was invited to one of the most beautiful church weddings that he had ever seen. The Preacher keeps telling me that we need to keep praying for our loved ones regardless of how hopeless the situation looks. We must learn that sin has got to run its course in their life for them to be willing to change. I asked him to please explain this and he replied with a gleam in his eye that we got to get to the place that we hate sin and what it can do to us. He said a Christian may fall into sin at a weak moment but they will not enjoy it and certainly not pursue it. Their nature has been changed and they no longer indulge in the things they used to love to do. For now, they find that the things they once hated they now love and the things they once loved, they now hate. They have the love of God permeating their heart.

Romans 8:28

Romans 8:28

"And we know that all things work together for good to them that love God, to them who are the called according to his purpose."

Have you ever thought, "Why Me Lord" only to later discover the reason why? [Sometime, years later] Such was the time of one missionary whose ship was wrecked back in the days where the only communication devices were pin, paper, and bottle. His party was in dangerous waters and their greatest fear was realized not when they capsized, but rather when they happened upon an island inhabited by cannibals! Before they could realize it, the cannibals surrounded them. Their leader approached this missionary in charge. The missionary was able to communicate with the cannibal's leader for the dialect was similar to one he had already known. The missionary proceeded to convince the cannibals that he and his party were not worth eating, because they were tainted from their travels. The cannibal's leader was convinced as the missionary took out his pocketknife, raised his pants leg to cut apiece off and hand it to the cannibal. After several spits of disgust, the savage leader exclaimed in his native tongue, "You no good! You can go!" Soon after, the missionary party was rescued. The members finally gained enough stamina to question their leader of this miraculous deliverance asking, "How?" The missionary replied with **Romans 8:28.**

He then proceeded to tell them of the ordeal he had gone through some years before of losing his leg and gaining a "cork" one in its place. At the time of the loss he had questioned God, but now realized its value in time and place.

Such was the time The Preacher had been ministering in the dead of winter a Trucker's Chapel in Somewhere, PA with Chaplain Mercy.

Drivers were amazed at the "Words of Knowledge" manifesting God's presence through Paul. They escorted Paul out to his truck confirming his prophetic call, giving him the sense that his destiny was drawing near, bringing a reverential fear and well of Joy all at the same time! Part of this revelation was that God was going to send people across Paul's path that were going to be influenced by, as well as be instrumental in ushering in the "End Time" harvest. The Preacher left the truck stop and proceeded west on I-80. He stopped to fuel in Dubois, PA. Ice and snow were present. Paul slipped as he prepared to exit his truck. The previous martial arts training kicked in as he was looking for anything to avert the impending fall. During the fall, his hand reached for and managed to grab the door's armrest. The after-market cushion gave way to the weight of his body and he continued down, to his moment of embarrassment, lying on the ground. Paul's body had impacted a stationary yellow pole designed to keep trucks from running into the fuel pumps.

For a while he laid still on the ground mentally and physically assessing the damage. After determining that he was not injured very badly, he rose to fuel. The difference came later in Erie, PA when he put himself in a twisting motion by attempting to place his overnight bag on the floor behind the passenger seat. Suddenly, Paul felt his ribs give way and crack sending excruciating pain throughout his upper torso. The pain reached its climax when he finally reached Raphine, VA. He could not even let the truck idle, because of the vibrations. In tears and exhaustion he began to call on his friend. Paul reminded God of his faithfulness and the sacrifices he had made in the service of the cross.

Suddenly the truck started to shake without any natural reason why, and after the shaking ceased the level of pain decreased dramatically! The Preacher was then able to rest. Upon returning to Tennessee, the doctor discovered that Paul had broken three ribs. This placed him out of work.

Paul purchased a recliner for a place to sleep, rest, and recover from this ordeal. He was a little stressed over the loss of income during this period. Someone placed a computer with Internet at Paul's disposal to give him something to do while he was chair bound. They gave him basic instructions and asked him to please stay out of the chat rooms. Paul soon found himself in the chat rooms. Like a bee to pollen he became a member of an African American Christian room. Drawn to this room by the Spirit he was accepted and greatly appreciated, as Paul would write articles of faith and faithfulness. In one of these sessions the "Word of Knowledge" came forth into effect revealing to him that one of the participants, Miss Prosperity, was dealing with the dreaded disease HIV. She had contracted this from her former unscrupulous husband. The Holy Spirit caused Paul to get a burden of interceding for Miss Prosper. He asked her to become a part of his newly formed ministry. She graciously accepted to be a member and a prayer warrior.

Sometime later, after Paul was healed and returned to trucking, he made his way to the North East to personally lay hands on Miss Prosperity and pray for her. Her Pastor called Paul to thank him for his ministry towards her, seeing the difference it had made in her countenance. This Pastor also has a burden for street people, and had started a church made up of such (One of Paul's burdens as well, for he has also started a homeless ministry in Atlanta, GA.).

After nearly two years of perseverance prayer and much opposition from the enemy, Miss Prosperity has now been delivered from the symptoms of this dreaded disease. Her complexion has cleared up and she is now actively in rolled in school to obtain her high school diploma. She also has plans to pursue a college career. Miss Prosperity and her friend Miss Joy are still current prayer intercessors with Paul's ministry. Miss Prosperity is also in the process of writing a book about her life and how the Living God has used her to touch others.

Some years before Paul fell and broke his ribs, he had also injured his back while attempting to unload his truck.

This also had placed him out of work for some time, causing him to get behind on his bills. Paul had decided to pay his own medical bills since the company he was working for frowned on employees filing for workman's compensation. This incident also ushered in another miracle of God, and a demonstration of His power. It looked as if he was about to lose everything he had worked for and all hope was lost but Almighty God was working behind the scenes. Paul received a phone call from a friend who had been touched by the Lord in one of the services Paul had been ministering in. The friend was an owner operator who drove coast to coast. Time was his name. Time's business had been blessed and was flourishing. Circumstances came to pass that Time was on a run that would bring him through Tennessee. Before leaving the West Coast, the Lord had revealed to Time that Paul was in a financial bind. Late in the evening the phone rang at Paul's home. Time was reporting that he was at a nearby truck stop and that he needed to see Paul. Not one other person had come to Paul and asked about his need while he was off work. Constantly Paul was reminded from outside and inside sources of the delinquency of payments. The Preacher kept reminding himself that God was his source and not man. Paul reminded the Lord of His Word, as well as the service he had given Him over the years.

The peace of God descended down into Paul's spirit and he knew then that everything would be okay! True to the peace God had given Paul, Time placed a check in his hand for $2500.00. Time informed Paul that the Lord had revealed to him of his need while in California. The Romans "8:28" of all this is not only Miss Prosperity's healing and the internet ministry but also when Paul broke his ribs and was laid up for some time, God finished the healing of his back which was injured from some time before.

Sometimes we just do not understand, until we go through suffering, to see the Glory that God makes. What the devil intends for bad God turns into good. Our suffering brings us patience and certainly gives us experience to help mold our character and to be able to help a brother or sister who is going through a tough trial and is about ready to give up on all hope. We can experience the joy of the Lord even in our storm by just knowing he is there and we cannot be lonely for we are surrounded by the family of God. We not only have the peace of God but we as his children have peace with God.

Proverbs 10:22

"The blessing of the LORD, it maketh rich, and he addeth no sorrow with it."

Conclusion

There are many other similar encounters we could relate in this novel and plan to in upcoming volumes.

Our novel exploiting the character of Paul the Trucker Evangelist is written to inspire everyone who reads it to seek and enter into a relationship with God; to experience His desires deeply manifested in their own lives. We undertook the task of writing this novel as a means of witness to others, the difference Jesus Christ can make in anyone's life, in the hope that others may find the secrets of living with and in Him. Pressing beyond the veil into the most Holy of Holies, we are praying for God's Spirit to communicate with you in a greater manner than ever before, as a result of reading this novel. May God also dispatch a ministering angel with each book published, with the assignment to accomplish this task. ***A-Men***

We can all learn to trust God as The Preacher has and be blessed in ways too numerous to comprehend.

Now To you, my Christian family:

The LORD bless thee, and keep thee: The LORD make His face shine upon thee, and be gracious unto thee: The LORD lift up His countenance upon thee, and give thee peace.

To you, who have not yet entered into a relationship (thru salvation) with Jesus Christ as savior and Lord:

As it is written, There is none righteous, no, not one: There is none that understandeth; there is none that seeketh after God. They are all gone out of the way, they are together become unprofitable; there is none that doeth good, no, not one. Their throat is an open sepulcher; with their tongues they have used deceit; the poison of asps is under their lips: Whose mouth is full of cursing and bitterness? Their feet are swift to shed blood: Destruction and misery are in their ways: And the way of peace have they not known: There is no fear of God before their eyes. For all have sinned, and come short of the glory of God; Therefore being justified by faith, we have peace with God through our Lord Jesus Christ:

By whom also we have access by faith into this grace wherein we stand, and rejoice in hope of the glory of God. But God commendeth His love toward us, in that, while we were yet sinners, Christ died for us. Much more then, being now justified by His blood, we shall be saved from wrath through Him For the wages of sin is death; but the gift of God is eternal life through Jesus Christ our Lord.

But what saith it? The word is nigh thee, even in thy mouth, and in thy heart: that is, the word of faith, which we preach;

That if thou shalt confess with thy mouth the Lord Jesus, and shalt believe in thine heart that God hath raised Him from the dead, thou shalt be saved.

For with the heart man believeth unto righteousness; and with the mouth confession is made unto salvation. For the scripture saith, whosoever believeth on Him shall not be ashamed. For there is no difference between the Jew and the Greek: for the same Lord. For whosoever shall call upon the name of the Lord shall be saved.

Friend, will you now after reading this novel, call out to a living Jesus? Confess your sins to Him and ask Him into your heart to be your Lord and Savior, for He says: *Behold, I stand at the door, and knock: if any man hear my voice, and open the door, I will come in to him, and will sup with him, and he with me"*

Let it be known, although this novel is written as a fictional work, the stories and events mentioned in it are factual and can be proven. Our main character, The Preacher is a real person who has been a professional driver for over thirty years. He was also used of the Lord to Found and Charter a real ministry and actually experienced all the events mentioned in this novel. In the coming future, there are plans for two more volumes on the life of this preacher as he will suffer more hardships and overcome all of them by the grace of the Living God.

Special Prayer

Dear Lord I come to you this day through, and in Jesus' name and in His shed blood, recognizing His great sacrifice at Calvary. I pray LORD, that your honor & glory be manifested in this work. May your countenance smile through it: to strengthen the redeemed, and add souls to your kingdom. LORD, I ask that your hand be upon it and may the HOLY SPIRIT'S presence anoint this work! Father, I ask you, to charge your ministering angels as posted guards, removing any hindrances that would come against this work. God... I pray you use this work to show people that you are the unchanging God. Your word declares it, that what you were yesterday, you are today, and will be tomorrow! Again LORD may Your Hand be upon this, in Jesus' name I pray! **Amen!"**

Hebrews 13:8

"Jesus Christ is the same yesterday and today and forever".

Remember, "They that labor to bring sunshine into the lives of others, cannot keep it from themselves"

Be Blessed and Be a Blessing!

Finally, a special note to the one minister who answered the call of God after graduating from Bible College about fifty years ago to minister on the highways, Chaplain Jim Keys. Chaplain Jim had persevered ten long years before he was blessed with his first convert, and his ministries. "Transport for Christ" and "The Association of Christian Truckers") have had many converts since. May God continue to richly bless his efforts!! AMEN! I do not want to leave out a special tribute to the late Chaplains Joe and Kris Tackit who left all to serve as ACT Chaplains under the ministry of Chaplain Jim Keys.

Please take a moment to visit the ACT web site listed for you. *http://www.acti70.org*

Made in the USA
Charleston, SC
11 June 2015